SHET

FOLK TALES

Shetland Folk Tales

Lawrence Tulloch

Illustrated by
Alexa Fitzgibbon

First published 2014
Reprinted 2016, 2019

The History Press
97 St George's Place, Cheltenham,
Gloucestershire, GL50 3QB
www.thehistorypress.co.uk

British Library Cataloguing in Publication Data.
A catalogue record for this book is available from the British Library.

ISBN 978 0 7524 9769 3

Typesetting and origination by The History Press
Printed in Great Britain by TJ Books Limited, Padstow, Cornwall

Contents

Acknowledgements

In compiling a book of stories it is not just the folk that you learned the stories from who have to be thanked. There are also the folk, long gone, who took the stories on during their lifetime.

My father, Tom Tulloch, was a major source of stories for me. He learned the stories from his mother and she got them from her father. Any storyteller will say much the same thing.

As well as the Henderson men, regular visitors to our house were Andrew Williamson from a house called The Brake. My Uncle Bobby from Brough told me about the sheep thief, Black Eric of Fitful Head.

When we lived in Gutcher, also in Yell, we were close to the ferry terminal and Jeemsie Laurenson from Fetlar never missed an opportunity of visiting when he was waiting for the ferry back home.

Jackie Renwick the poet and storyteller from Unst we saw several times a week when he was working in Yell. Although he was never a visitor to our house I had the privilege of hearing the great Brucie Henderson from Arisdale in Yell tell stories.

Gordon Walterson from Sandness is another who has given me stories. Charlie Laurenson from Voe is yet another. We used to go to meetings together and he was always at his best in a one to one.

Although he is no longer a young man, George P.S. Peterson from Papa Stour and Brae is still Shetland's premier storyteller. He has a huge number of stories and he was a founder member of the Scottish Storytellers Forum.

Some of my best friends are fellow storytellers and they have made a big contribution to my store of stories: Hjorlefur Helga

Stefenson from Iceland, I never see him often enough, and Ian Stephan from Lewis who has been my friend for many years.

Bob Pegg has invited me to many festivals and gatherings. He is a man with awesome talent and personality and it was he who suggested that I write this book. His own book, in this series, is superb.

I am an only child but there is one who I look on as a brother. He is Tom Muir from Orkney. Together we have clocked up thousands of miles on storytelling adventures. No man could ever be a better or more generous companion.

I greatly value the friendship and encouragement that I have received from Professor Bo Almqvist. He is from Sweden but he lives in Dublin. I regard him as the foremost authority on Nordic folklore and legends.

Thanks also to Northmavine men Peter Robertson and Ivor Johnson. Peter lent me some books and both of them have followed my progress and they have put me on the track of stories. I am grateful to The History Press and Declan Flynn for giving me this writing opportunity.

As always I am indebted to my family for the help and support they have given me. Margaret, my wife, has been with me every step of the way, as she is with all my endeavours. Without her this book would never have happened.

Our daughter, Liz, has been very involved in the writing of this book. Her computer skills, the time and patience she has given; it has been of the utmost help. She has also been my researcher and advisor. Just when I thought that something was impossible she would come up with the answer.

Last but not least I thank Alexa Fitzgibbon. Despite her name she is French and she came to Shetland, as a student, in 2006. Since then we have come to look on her as part of our family and, to me, she is like another daughter. Despite on-going poor health she agreed to illustrate this book and I could not be more pleased. She has brought a wonderful enchantment to it.

Writing is said to be a lonely occupation, but not this time: I have had so much encouragement and support. Sincere thanks to everyone who has helped me.

Introduction

When my great friend Bob Pegg suggested that I write this book, my first reaction was to ask myself if I knew enough stories that I had not already published. When I sat down with a notebook and pen I was pleasantly surprised at the list I compiled.

There were also many stories that I knew in part. I had heard the stories told but did not know them well enough to attempt to tell them to an audience.

I was extraordinarily lucky in my young life, to meet and hear so many wonderful storytellers. During my youth we lived in three different houses and each one seemed to be a magnet for interesting visitors.

Shetland, at the latitude 60 degrees north, has long dark winter nights, which are ideal to visit and welcome visitors alike. In my childhood and youth we had no electricity and therefore no television, no phone – computers were unheard of. We did have a radio but it worked off a combination of wet and dry batteries. The dry batteries were expensive and the wet battery had to be recharged on a regular basis, so it was not surprising that the radio was used sparingly.

What we did have was books and visitors providing fantastic conversation that often expanded into storytelling. Good stories did not have to be epic folk tales, it might be no more than someone telling of a trip to the shop.

With no streetlights and pitch-dark evenings, those going out on a visit would take with them a burning peat from the fire. It would be carried in tongs or speared on a stiff wire. Outside in the fresh air and wind it would burn bright and show them the way.

If it was still burning when they reached their destination they would put the peat in the host's fire. When going home again the reverse would be the case. In the wintertime when a household had invited visitors it was referred to as having folk 'in aboot da nite'.

Families and friends were invited to spend an evening and later the visit would be returned. Many a time there were visitors who just called in on the spur of the moment. To visit each other was one of the ways of shortening the long winter nights.

My father, Tom Tulloch, was to be found in his workshop almost every evening. He was a wood worker and a metal worker and he often made doors, windows, wheelborrows, threshing machines, harrows, rollers and much more for friends and neighbours.

Shetland is a treeless place but in those days wood was plentiful; it came from the sea from ships sunk or damaged during the Second World War. Money seldom changed hands but anyone that my father worked for would do something for him in return.

He also had a circular saw that was driven by an old engine that started life in a car. Wood would be sawn into boards or however it was wanted but much of it was rough wood and was made into fencing posts.

Every night he had visitors in his workshop, some were there to help while others came for the crack and many stories were told, some of them were of the 'after 9 p.m. variety', and I wish I had paid more attention.

At this time, the Henderson brothers, John and Bertie, were regular visitors to our house. They lived in the most isolated part of the island, a place called West-A-Firth; it had no road to it and anyone going to it, or coming from it, on a winter's night had to tackle a formidable journey through moorland and mire. No one locked their doors in those days and it was no uncommon thing to get up in the morning to find John sleeping in the resting chair beside the fire. If he had been somewhere and did not fancy the long walk home he never hesitated to come to our house, the Haa of Midbrake, to await daylight.

If the weather was really bad he might stay for several days and he was always a welcome visitor. I have travelled a good deal and

I have heard scores of storytellers but none that could hold a candle to John and Bertie. When they described someone they had the knack, like a cartoonist, of making the exaggeration that brought them to life. John was also a master mimic who could reproduce the voice and mannerisms of anyone that he heard speaking or saw moving.

They never were aware of it but every time that they spoke they gave a masterclass in storytelling. Some of the things they said might, nowadays, be considered politically incorrect but it was said entirely free from either spite or malice. It is they and many others who have inspired this book.

Lawrence Tulloch, 2014

1

The Fetlar Finnman

Fetlar is the fourth largest island in Shetland. It is very fertile and is sometimes known as the Garden of Shetland. Nonetheless, Fetlar folk depended on the sea for part of their living, as did other Shetland communities.

Fetlar has no natural harbour so the boats used for fishing had to be small enough, and light enough, that they could be hauled up the beach after every fishing trip. While many men worked together and went to the fishing as a crew, one young man tended to fish alone.

Erty prided himself on being the best fisherman in Fetlar and he went to sea in some very rough and stormy seas. The older men advised him to be more careful but he was entirely confident and he paid no heed to what they said.

On one really bad day, so bad that even Erty was compelled to stay on the shore, he met a Finnman on the road. Finnmen were a race of creatures that lived in the sea. They could take any form that they wished and sometimes they lived on floating islands that were invisible to the human eye. On the shore they were usually seen as tall dark, handsome men, always well dressed and rich.

The Finnman greeted Erty and said, 'You think that you are a great fisherman but I will wager that there will be no fresh fish on your table this side of Jül.'

This was like showing a red rag to a bull. Erty bristled and was more than ready to meet the challenge. In the days that followed, the weather never relented and no fishing was possible. Erty was not too worried because Jül was some way off.

The wind blew and blew from the southeast, the worst possible direction, and even when it shifted it was never for long enough to allow the heavy seas to settle down. Erty was on the alert day and night looking for any weather window.

He had almost given up hope when, on Tammasmas Day, five days before Jül, the wind suddenly eased and went into the west. The next morning he was up long before dawn and with the first greek of day he decided that it was now or never. He knew enough about the weather to be fully aware that the lull would be no more than just that, a lull.

He put his tackle in the boat but he had no bait. It was a high tide and there was not so much as a limpet to be had from the rocks. To go without bait was a waste of time, and then he had a desperate idea.

His wife had bought linen to make clothes from and he knew that there were a number of off-cuts. He went home and got some of those and carefully wrapped strips of linen around the hooks.

He took his razor-sharp knife and made a deep cut in one of his fingers. It bled profusely and he soaked the linen on the hooks with blood. This done he lost no time in launching the boat and rowing away from the shore. He also took with him the pig, the earthenware jar in which they gathered fish livers. (Liver oil was used for the lamps and for lubricating wool that was going to be spun into yarn.) Erty knew that the liver oil could calm the sea, and given that his adventure was dangerous he felt that the oil might prove useful.

Conditions were far from ideal and but for the wager with the Finnman he would never have ventured out that day. He went directly to the nearest place where he was likely to catch a fish. He did not care what sort of a fish he caught; anything would do, so long as he could prove the Finnman wrong.

His line had been in the water for no more than a minute when he felt the strong tug of a fish on it. To his delight it was a cod, not the biggest cod he had ever caught but it would be a meal to him and his wife, and the Finnman was beaten.

As soon as he had the fish safely in the boat he made all speed for the shore but the weather was getting worse by the minute. Facing the stern of the boat he could see three enormous seas building, waves that were out of character even with this rough day.

The first wave ran under the boat and did no real damage but the second one nearly swamped the boat, and Erty knew that he had no chance of surviving the third. He remembered the liver oil and he poured some of it on the water; it had some effect but the big wave seemed to be unstoppable.

Erty stood up in the boat and with all his strength he hurled the pig, oil and all, into the face of the wave. The wave faltered, it seemed to stop and then it died down to be no bigger than any of the other waves.

By this time, Erty was close to the beach and his neighbours had heard that he had gone to the sea and they were there to look for him to try to help. As soon as the boat touched the beach, willing hands grabbed it and carried it up the beach and beyond the reach of the angry sea.

Erty had to endure several lectures from the older men but he took the cod home and it made a delicious meal for him and his wife. It was a few days after that when he met the Finnman again but this time Erty scarcely recognised him; he had a black eye, his nose was broken and some of his teeth were missing. Undaunted, Erty reminded him of the wager. The Finnman snarled at him and said through the teeth that he had left, 'You are getting nothing from me. You spewed out that filthy oil and you struck me in the face with that stinking jar.'

Erty never saw the Finnman again.

2

The Netted Mermaid

Fishing with long lines was labour intensive and very hard work and not least because bait was required for every one of the four hundred or so hooks on each line. Herring and mackerel were used but time had to be spent in catching them.

The skipper of one boat decided to experiment with nets. He reasoned that they could set a few nets and fish while the nets were left to collect the desired fish. On one occasion when they came to hail the net they could feel something heavy in it.

They pulled the net in alongside the boat and they were astonished to find that they had caught a mermaid. She was terrified and she was crying in an uncontrollable manner. Her long golden hair was woven into the net as well as her fish tail.

When she looked into the boat her eyes met the eyes of one of the youngest members of the crew.

'Help me Magnie, please help me,' she pleaded.

Young Magnie's father, Geordie, was the skipper and he gave his son a fierce look.

'Do you know this creature, boy?' he demanded to know.

Magnie just nodded. The crew pulled the mermaid into the boat and she was freed from the net. Geordie looked angry.

'Will someone tell me what is going on?'

Magnie had difficulty finding speech and so the mermaid spoke:

'One evening when I was sitting on a rock Magnie came close to me. Maybe I was sleeping but I never heard him or knew that he was there until he put his arms around me. He is very handsome and like every mermaid my dearest wish is to be married to human man.

'After that we met many times and I learned to speak the human tongue. I have fallen in love with Magnie, it is a love that will never die. I know that Magnie feels the same way about me but my father will not allow us to get married.

'Only he has the power to take away this fish's tail and give me the legs of an earthly woman. He wants me to marry a human but he wants it to be to a rich man not a poor fisherman.

'We had a serious quarrel this morning and I had to flee for my life. My father is an evil man and he would rather kill me than allow me to marry Magnie and he will certainly kill Magnie if he ever gets the chance. It was because I was in a panic that I swam into your net.'

Some of the men wanted to put the mermaid back into the sea and old Geordie was somewhat hostile too. Magnie spoke for the first time.

'Father, if you put Mara back into the sea you will be sending her to her death and I will not have that; I will go with her and I will die too.'

Geordie knew that his son was determined and meant what he said so, reluctantly, he consented to taking Mara ashore with them. Magnie's mother had to be told and though she did not like the situation, there was not much that she could do.

One of the first things that Mara noticed in the fishermen's house was the cross that hung on the wall. It was made of iron, roughly made by Magnie when he was apprentice to the local blacksmith, and the two pieces of metal had been walled. They had been heated and hammered together to form a join. The rest of the cross had also been hammered so that it had dozens of facets.

Years of polishing gave it a deep, burnished shine and for Magnie's mother it was her most precious possession. As one who had been brought up to hate Christianity, Mara felt uncomfortable with it but she said nothing.

When Mara and Magnie were alone they discussed the situation and Magnie was in no doubt that the merman, Mara's father, had to be confronted. Mara kept telling him that he had no idea how powerful and how evil her father really was.

She said that his power came from the knife that he always carried. She knew that without the knife he was no threat to anyone but, hard as she had tried, she had never been able to steal the knife from him. He slept with it under his pillow and during the day he wore it in his belt.

It was with the knife that he intended to kill one or both of them. Mara said that they would never be safe from him because he would patrol the shore tirelessly until he found them.

'Right,' said Magnie, 'I will go to the shore now and have it out with him.'

He ignored her protests and set out for the beach, unarmed except for one secret weapon. He did not have long to wait before the merman appeared. With a face that was full of hatred he said through clenched teeth, 'You have destroyed my daughter's life, earthman, and for that you will pay with your life.'

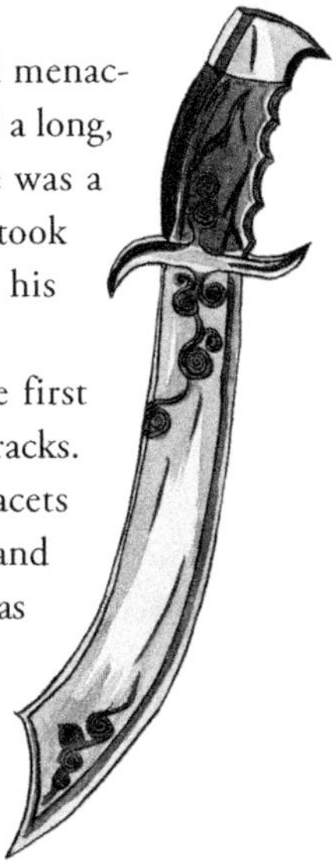

He drew the magic knife and moved forward menacingly and with murder in his heart. The knife had a long, curved and wicked-looking blade. But Magnie was a brave young man, and he stood his ground. He took the cross belonging to his mother from under his gansy and held it aloft.

The cross caught the sunlight and when the first ray shone in the merman's face he halted in his tracks. Magnie kept the cross moving and the many facets reflected the light, leaving the merman blinded and shaken. He staggered back and fell, but Magnie was unrelenting. He kept the light shining into the merman's face and the merman began to shrink in size, his knife falling from his powerless hand.

Magnie picked the knife up and threatened the merman, 'You were determined to kill me and you deserve to die. But I am not as evil or wicked as you are so I will not take your life. Go back to the sea before I change my mind and if I ever see you again it will be worse for you.'

The merman scuttled down the beach and disappeared beneath the waves and a new sound came to Magnie's ears. It was Mara laughing and running down the path and into Magnie's arms. She no longer had the fish tail, instead she had lovely slender legs; she was stunningly beautiful and Magnie was even more in love with her.

Soon they were married and went to live in their own house. Magnie left the sea to take over from his mentor as the village blacksmith, which gave him more time to spend with Mara and their three children, two boys and a girl.

As for the omnipotent merman's knife – Magnie took it home. Mara was given her own cross as a wedding present; it was fashioned by Magnie in the forge from the evil knife that the merman once owned. Mara polished it every day and it hung in their cottage in a place where, on bright mornings, it reflected the early sun and filled the room with gladness.

3

The Laughing Merman

A lone fisherman was rather sad because he was having no luck: he had been fishing all morning and he had shifted to a number of fishing grounds but without any luck.

He was sure his luck had changed when he felt a big weight on his line and very powerful tugging. He hauled with all his might and was amazed and somewhat dismayed when he discovered that he had hooked a merman.

The merman was small and ugly, and when he was hauled into the boat he was very angry. He demanded to be released and allowed to go back into the sea. The fisherman told him that he would be taken ashore.

'You don't look as if you will be for any use but I have caught nothing else so I will keep you for the time being and I will not release you until it suits me to do so.' And he put the merman into a basket and secured the top so that he could not escape. By this time it was late afternoon and the fisherman decided that he had been at sea long enough, so he took in his lines and made for the shore.

The fisherman's wife was there to meet him; she put her arms around him and told him how much she loved him, and at the same time the dog came to greet him but he kicked the dog and told him to go home. The merman laughed loudly.

As they walked up the path to the cottage the fisherman tripped over an embedded stone and he nearly fell on his face. The merman laughed loudly again. Later, some peddlers came to the house and among the things that they had for sale were boots and shoes.

The fisherman refused to buy any because he said that the soles were too thin and that they would not last long. The peddler

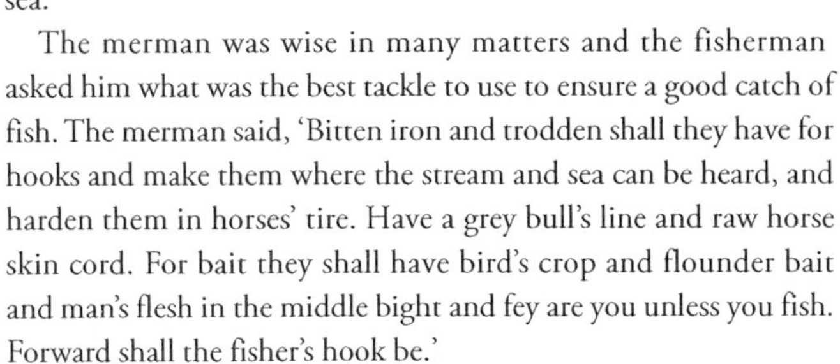

showed him that the soles were double thick but again the fisherman insisted that they were too thin. The merman laughed loudly. Inside the house the fisherman demanded to know why the merman laughed, but he would say nothing.

The merman was kept a prisoner for three days and nights, with the fisherman trying to force him to explain what he was laughing at. The merman said that he would let the fisherman know, but only if he was taken back to the place where he was caught, to be released. At last they came to a compromise. The merman agreed to tell the fisherman if he was allowed to sit on the blade of an oar that was outstretched from the boat above the sea.

The merman was wise in many matters and the fisherman asked him what was the best tackle to use to ensure a good catch of fish. The merman said, 'Bitten iron and trodden shall they have for hooks and make them where the stream and sea can be heard, and harden them in horses' tire. Have a grey bull's line and raw horse skin cord. For bait they shall have bird's crop and flounder bait and man's flesh in the middle bight and fey are you unless you fish. Forward shall the fisher's hook be.'

The fisherman then wanted to know why the merman laughed when his wife and dog met him at the beach.

'I laughed because you are so stupid. The dog loves you and he is your best friend but you kicked him. Your wife loves another man and wants you dead but you kissed and caressed her.

'The stone that you cursed lies on top of a pot of gold that would make you rich but you are so stupid that you do not know this. I laughed when you would not buy the shoes because you are so stupid that you do not know they would have lasted all the rest of your life. You have only three more days to live.'

The merman dived off the oar and disappeared into the sea but everything that he said turned out to be true and a poem was written to remember this event:

> Well I mind that morning
> merman laughed so low;
> wife to wait her husband
> water's edge did go;
> kissed him there so kindly,
> cold her heart as snow;
> beat his dog so blindly,
> barked his joy to show.

4

The Mermaid Who Loved a Fisherman

Once upon a time there was a mermaid who fell in love with a fisherman. The fisherman was poor and the mermaid's father would not allow her to marry the fisherman, but it was only her father who had the power to free her from the fish's tail that was her lower body.

He tried to persuade her to look for a rich man, one who would keep her with plenty for the rest of her life. She said no, she wanted no one save the young fisherman. They sat together near the sea whenever they had the opportunity and dreamed of being married and having children.

Her father came to realise that no matter what he said his daughter would never leave the fisherman. One night when the lovers met, the mermaid had the startling news that her father had decided that the only way that he could break the romance was to kill the fisherman. The mermaid produced a knife and handed it to the fisherman.

'This is the knife that he would kill you with,' she said. 'Keep it safe because it is no ordinary knife. But just because I have stolen it from him does not mean that you are safe. He has great powers and he will brew up a great storm and use that to sink your boat. When this looks like happening you must throw the knife into the sea and that will calm the billows.'

The fisherman was far from convinced but he accepted the knife, and to please her he promised to do as she said. The very next day the mermaid watched from her favourite place on the shore as her

lover sailed his boat out to the fishing grounds.

He had only been fishing for a short time when the sky began to darken and the wind began to blow hard. The gentle swell turned into big, breaking waves and the boat was tossed around like a piece of cork.

Waves began to break over the boat and the mermaid knew that the boat had to be filling with water and was in grave danger of sinking. She also knew that the storm was the evil work of her father, and willed and implored the fisherman to throw the knife into the sea.

When he did not she thought that maybe he had forgotten about it so she slipped into the water and swam off to the boat as fast as she could. She was going to shout above all the noise and urge him to throw the knife.

But the fisherman suddenly remembered the knife and what the mermaid had told him, so he threw it into the raging sea. By this time the mermaid was near the boat and the knife plunged deep into her beautiful white breast, killing her instantly.

And so it was that the fisherman lost the love of his life, the merman had lost his only daughter and neither of them was ever happy again.

5

The Blacksmith and the Njuggel

A njuggel is a creature that no community wants to have. Njuggels usually live in freshwater lochs, they can take on any form they want but, more often than not, they look like a horse.

Discerning folk can nearly always know a njuggel if they meet with one. A njuggel's coat is never dry and the hair grows upwards, the opposite way from an ordinary horse. A njuggel will sometimes, on a cold, dark and stormy night, stand by the roadside and invite a weary traveller to ride on its back. But anyone foolish enough to take up the offer will always regret it. The njuggel is unlikely to take them anywhere that they want to go and, if they ever reach home, they will find that their clothes have a horrible smell, are soaking wet and can never be dried.

However, it is children that are most in danger from the njuggel. A njuggel's tail is very long tail and it can shape it into a wheel of sorts, which can spin around. Children find this most attractive and the njuggel will invite a child to sit on it for a ride.

Any child who sits on a njuggel's tail is doomed; the njuggel will take the child into the loch never to be seen again. On one island the njuggel had preyed on so many children that very few were left.

One who had so far managed to elude the njuggel was the blacksmith's daughter. She was an early teenager, and she was big and strong like her father, and she had eluded the njuggel despite all his efforts to capture her.

Eventually the patience of the njuggel was exhausted so he took a direct approach. He arrived at the blacksmith's forge full of menace and in a wicked temper. He demanded that the blacksmith hand over his daughter saying that if he refused he would be killed. The blacksmith stood his ground, looked the njuggel in the eye and said, 'You will never have my daughter. She is all I have, especially since her mother died. She is the apple of my eye and I defend her with my life.'

The njuggel's face went black with rage and he stamped his hoofs on the ground.

'I will give you one last chance,' he said. 'I will come back in twenty-four hours and if you hand over the girl well and good but if you still refuse I will kill you and take her anyway.'

Twenty-four hours gave the blacksmith time to prepare and he told his daughter what he planned to do and what he wanted her to do. That done, he set about making some special thick, extra heavy horse shoes for a very special horse.

The njuggel duly arrived the next day and repeated his demand and was met with the same answer. To demonstrate his power the njuggel reared up before bringing his hoofs down with a mighty crash that shook the building.

'Next time those hoofs will come down on you head,' he roared.

The njuggel reared up again, higher than ever, with deadly intent. He was almost perpendicular when the blacksmith made his move. The njuggel was used to people backing away from him in fear so he was unprepared for what happened next.

Instead of back away, the blacksmith charged forward and caught the njuggel on the point of balance. He was a big, strong fit man and with all his might he put both hands on the njuggel's belly and pushed the njuggel over.

The njuggel fell backwards to the floor and got jammed stuck tight, between the anvil and the workbench. He was unable to get up and all four legs were waving in the air. The girl came from her hiding place and sat down on the njuggel's head and for once in his wicked life he was helpless.

The blacksmith had everything ready and he lost no time in nailing the heavy horseshoes to the njuggel's hooves. With his expert eye he had sized up the njuggel's feet, and the shoes fitted perfectly.

Once the blacksmith had finished and the shoes were secure on the njuggel's hooves, the blacksmith allowed it to stand up again.

But now it was a very different njuggel, gone were the threats and bragging. Instead it was a pathetic, timid and shivering creature.

An evil creature like the njuggel cannot abide iron and now he was nailed to iron shoes forever more. He could not even go into the loch again because the heavy shoes weighted him down. The njuggel was now harmless, never a threat to any child again. It is said that the story of the blacksmith and the njuggel is where the tradition of horse shoes being good luck comes from.

6

MARTHA

There is a village on the island of Yell called the Herra. It can be found near the middle of the island sandwiched between the west coast and the shores of Whale Firth. A young lady called Martha Mann lived there and she was very well known in the area.

She was expert in healing sick animals. If anyone had a sick cow, horse or sheep it was to Martha that they went for help. She seldom failed but sometimes it was hard to understand how her medicine worked and her methods had never been seen before.

There were whispers that she used witchcraft but no one ever made that accusation openly. That would have been a very serious charge perhaps resulting in a trial and besides, Martha had never done anything to harm any person or animal. On the contrary, she had done a great deal to help people.

An elderly woman walked from Gossabrough, on the other side of the island, about eight miles away, to enlist Martha's help. It was a considerable undertaking for the woman, walking across trackless moorland, but she was at her wits' end; her cow could not eat or chew the cud, it would not even drink water and had become so weak that it could not stand up. It just lay in the byre near to death.

Martha told the woman that she was sorry but she could not go with her to Gossabrough. She was very busy and she had promised to help two other folk with sick animals. But she invited the woman into her cottage and gave her some food and drink.

While the woman was eating, Martha went into another room of the house and came back with a pocket-sized square of thick felted cloth and handed it to the woman. When the woman looked

at it more closely she saw that it was, in fact, two squares sewn together. In the middle was something round and hard, perhaps a small stone, but there was no opening and no way into this bag without cutting the stitches.

'Tie this around the cow's horn and it should help, but please bring it back tomorrow because I am likely to need it,' said Martha.

The woman made her way home through the hills feeling rather disappointed. She had banked her hopes on Martha Mann and now felt that her long journey to the Herra was a waste of time. She had no faith whatsoever in the square of cloth in her pocket, no matter what it contained.

When she got home she went into the byre and her precious cow was even weaker than when she left. The hay and water remained untouched and it did not look as though the cow had long to live.

She tied the cloth to the cow's horn as Martha suggested. By this time though it was quite late and she was very tired so she went into her small house and went to bed. It was a measure of her tiredness that she slept until morning but as soon as she wakened she threw a shawl around her shoulders and went straight to the byre to see if the cow was still alive.

She was amazed to hear the cow mooing contently and even more amazed to see the cow on her feet. She had eaten all the hay and drunk all the water and seemed to be restored to full health and strength.

The woman saw the fully recovered cow as a miracle and she remembered her promise to return the square of cloth to Martha. However, she was simply too tired; the sixteen-mile walk the previous day had taken its toll and she reasoned that surely Martha would manage without the cloth for another day.

She spent most of the day with her cow, hardly able to believe that she had made a full recovery. The following morning she made preparations for returning to the Herra but when she went to retrieve the square of cloth from the cow's horn she found, to her dismay, that it was empty.

The stitching around all four sides was intact but it was flat – empty. She took the cloth, put it in her pocket and set out, not knowing what to say to Martha. It was a beautiful sunny, warm day and when she reached the Herra, Martha was sitting outside her cottage enjoying the sunshine.

She tried to tell Martha about the cloth and the fact that the contents had vanished but Martha stopped her.

'There is nothing to worry about,' she said. 'I did need that yesterday so I fetched it back. It is not lost at all.' When this story became public, everyone in the village suspected that Martha was a witch, though no one would utter it out loud.

Martha herself was not happy, she was acutely lovesick. She was madly in love with Andrew Grott, the young man who worked in the village shop. He was handsome, cheerful and popular with all the customers, and Martha made many trips to the shop to speak to him. Though he always treated her with great courtesy, it was abundantly clear that he was in no way interested in her romantically.

She never gave up, but none of her feminine wiles had the slightest effect on him. It was a stalemate: the routine of the village going on the way it had always done. It was summer time and the fishing boats were going off to sea every day to distant fishing grounds, even as far as the edge of the continental shelf.

The boats used in those days were called sixtreens (an open boat around thirty-feet long) and as the name suggests they were manned by six men. They were open boats and with calm weather or head winds they were rowed but when the wind was favourable they hoisted a square sail in the fashion of their Viking ancestors.

Late one afternoon a man came into the shop but he did not want to buy anything, he wanted to talk to Andrew Grott. The man was Lowry Tarrel and he was the veteran skipper of one of the boats. No man on the island had more knowledge or more experience of the sea. He told Andrew that one of his crew was sick and asked if Andrew would be willing to go to sea with them to fill the gap. Andrew was very pleased; he liked his job in the shop but a day or two fishing out at sea would be a nice change.

The morning dawned bright and fair but when they were out of the firth and in the open sea they saw something that unsettled them; three huge waves coming at them like wild animals, each one more powerful than the last.

Andrew Grott said, 'In the name of the Lord what mountains of sea is this?'

'Pay no attention to that while I'm aboard,' Tarrel told him. 'These three, that's no ordinary waves, this sea is from the wicked one!'

Andrew declared that the boat would never get through this but Tarrel told him that he need not be frightened because he knew what to do.

The first wave made the boat shudder in every plank. They had just about recovered when the second one hit. It was bigger than the first and it half-filled the boat with seawater. Every one of the crew had to bale like madmen to try and get the water out. They knew that if the third struck they had no chance of surviving.

Without a word, Lowry Tarrel handed the helm to one of his crew and took hold of the huggie staff, the gaff that they used to bring big fish into the boat. He stood up and spoke as loudly and clearly as he could.

'Either in the name of God or in the name of the Devil, whatsoever manner o' thing you are, speak to us.'

The sea eased off and a shape came out of it. It look like a flayed bullock, it had no skin and the red flesh bulged with muscles, blue veins and was covered in places with yellow fat. The naked

head had bulging eyes and huge bare teeth. It managed to hook one leg over the gunwale of the boat and demanded: 'Give me out Andrew Grott.'

'If Andrew Grott goes out of the boat we all go out of the boat,' Tarrel said. 'This ship o' ours will never be destroyed so long as God is stronger than the Devil.'

So saying, he smote the leg of the monster a mighty blow and it slid out of the boat and disappeared into the depths of the ocean. The sea became tranquil again and Tarrel and his crew trimmed the boat and went on their way to the fishing grounds.

As it turned out they had a most successful trip, catching big fish that were in the very best condition, and their trip back to the Herra was without incident. At the shore most of the villagers were there to greet them and everyone was given a fish or two to make a tasty meal.

One person who was absent was Martha Mann. Lowry Tarrel noticed this and asked if there was a reason why she was not there. He was told that she had had an accident, she had been trying to climb over a wall, a stone had fallen on her and she had a broken leg. She was indoors with her leg in splints.

The following day, Lowry Tarrel made his way to the shop again but not as a customer, he wanted to talk to Andrew Grott in private. He said, 'I strongly advise you, Andrew, never to go to sea again. It will be very dangerous for you. Yesterday I was with you and I knew what to do and say. This will be my last season at the fishing and another less experienced skipper might not be able to handle a similar situation. Stay ashore, Andrew, stay ashore for your own good.'

At the end of the summer, Lowry Tarrel did, indeed, retire, and Andrew Grott continued to work in the shop and Martha Mann, now recovered from her broken leg, continued her attempts to woo him but still without success.

Andrew either forgot or ignored Tarrel's advice, because when he was asked to stand in for a fisherman who was ill he readily agreed. This time the sixtreen did not return. Other boats fishing in the same area did not see them and they experienced no bad weather.

The wind was moderate and the sea was calm. It was hoped that, for some reason, they had landed on another island but no one had seen them. Eventually family and friends had to accept that they had been lost even if it was impossible to understand.

Another fishing season came to an end and the gloom caused by the loss of the sixtreen that Andrew was in hung heavily over the entire community, and with the dark nights of the winter came rumours that ghosts had been seen. Several folk had seen a number of ghostly figures and as the accounts grew more frequent, many were afraid to go out in the darkness, especially by themselves. One man that was never timid was John Smollett. He was a man of forty or so, a big man and one who was renowned for his prodigious strength.

John lived with his two sisters and his eighty-year-old father, Francis. Also sharing their home were two lambs, too frail to be outside during the harsh Shetland winter. While the folk had their supper of porridge or broth the lambs were given a few handfuls of hay to keep them quiet during the night.

John went out to get hay but came back into the kitchen without any hay for the lambs and looking upset.

'I cannot go out there,' he said. His father could guess what John had seen. He pulled on a pair of clogs and went outside and when his eyes adjusted to the darkness he could make out a huddle of weary men behind the haystack. He could see five men and a black dog.

'Speak now either in the name of God or in the name of the wicked one,' commanded Francis. There was no answer but he knew how to get them to speak.

'Is it ebbing or flowing?' asked Francis.

'You know it is flowing,' came back the answer.

'Is the moon waning or growing?'

A different voice answered.

'You know that it is waning.'

Francis then pointed to the black dog and asked, 'What kind of beast is this?'

After a pause the voice came back again. 'That thing can't mix with us as black can't mix with white. We have a story to tell and we cannot rest until it is told.'

This is the story they told: the day that they set sail with Andrew on board they met the same three waves as Tarrel and his crew, but the new skipper froze and he did none of the things that Tarrel did and they were overwhelmed by the third wave. One of those poor souls said, 'We have been around the earth ever since, we have not been in heaven or any other place but we know that our ship should never have been destroyed while God is stronger than the Devil.'

At that the black dog barked and flames came out of its jaws. It ran away; it ran and ran until it disappeared over the high cliffs. The crew of ghosts were calm now they walked away and Francis watched them disappear into the darkness.

And what of Martha Mann? The day after Francis Smollett talked to the ghosts she simply wasn't there anymore.

7

THE SEAL ON THE VEE SKERRIES

The Vee Skerries lie off the west coast of the Shetland Mainland and they are one of the most dangerous reefs in Shetland waters. Those cruel rocks have wrecked many ships and claimed the lives of many seafarers because they are submerged at high tide.

At low tide they are a favourite place for seals to rest and sunbathe. In the days when Shetlanders valued seals for their pelts and oil it was a place where seal hunters found rich pickings.

Once, a number of men from the nearby island of Papa Stour landed there to hunt, and one man was landed on a skerry, by himself. Without warning the wind got up to near gale force. With an incoming tide the sea became rough, and was soon very rough. The man was marooned. His friends came back with the boat but it proved impossible to get near enough for him to scramble on board.

To stay where they were was suicide for every one of them, so the boat had to stand off, hoping that the weather would ease quickly and enough for them to rescue their friend. Instead of getting better it got worse and the boat's crew had no option, they had to row for the shore while it was still possible.

The man on the skerry resigned himself to his fate. The tide was rising and before long he knew that it would cover the rock and he would be drowned. He noticed a seal swimming to and fro and watching him. Seals have expressive faces and he could see that this one was distressed.

At last the seal came really close to the rock and the man was astonished when it spoke.

'One of your friends clubbed my son to death and took his skin. They have it in the boat and I want it back.'

The man replied that he was marooned and there was nothing that he could do.

'I will make a bargain with you,' answered the seal. 'I will take you on my back and land you safely on the shore if you will make me a promise that you will give me my son's skin.'

The man agreed to this but he said that if the skin she wanted was not among the rest then it would be impossible for him to keep the promise. The seal was sure that the skin was one of the skins the men had taken.

'Lie face down on my back, put your arms around my neck and your legs at either side of my body as if you were riding a horse,' the seal ordered.

This was done and the seal left the Vee Skerries and, even though weighed down, made excellent progress towards Papa Stour. When they got to the beach the other men had already secured the boat and gone home.

The man told the seal to wait and he went to a shed where fish and fishing lines were kept. In there he found the dozens of seal skins that they had taken from the Vee Skerries but he did not know which skin the seal wanted.

He looked among them for a time and then he saw one that was more beautiful than the rest. He took this one and showed it to the seal. The seal confirmed that it was the skin that she wanted; she thanked the man and set off back to the sea. That man never hunted seals again.

8

MALLIE AND THE TROW

Mallie was a widow who lived with her three sons. They were all big healthy young men, and their mother found it very hard to feed them. They were very poor; money was in short supply since the man of the house had been lost at sea.

At the start of every winter they had a few potatoes, a small barrel of salted herrings and a boll (140lbs) of oatmeal. As the boys got bigger, Mallie found it harder and harder to make this scanty supply of food last all winter.

There came the time, the winter still had a distance to go, when the last of the herring was taken from the barrel and the last of the meal was taken from the girner. As they ate this frugal meal Mallie explained that they had no more food left and hungry days lay ahead.

The following day the boys were all as hungry as ever and there was no food.

'What are we going to do?' asked the oldest son.

'We shall have to become beggars, there is nothing else for it,' he was told.

The old woman who lived close by always seemed to have plenty of food, so the same boy volunteered to go and ask her. He knocked on her door and she came and answered it.

'All our food has been eaten, we are all going hungry, please can you give us something to eat?'

He could see into the kitchen of the house, he could see that the cupboard door was open and the shelves were laden with food. There was bread, cheese, cooked meat, oatmeal, flour, tea, coffee and jar after jar of jam and preserves; the cupboard was filled to overflowing.

The old woman gave the boy a withering look.

'Go away, how dare to come to my door begging, I have nothing to give you and do not come back or it will be worse for you.'

He came back home to his mother and his brothers, crying. He was a big boy and crying was for babies but he was so hungry and he could not understand how that woman could be so hard and unkind.

'Some folk are like that, son,' his mother said. 'Be pleased that we are different.'

Late in the afternoon a knock came to the door and standing on the doorstep was a little old man with grey hair and twinkling blue eyes but dressed in rags.

'Can you give me something to eat?' he asked. 'I have been on the road for two days without any food at all.'

Mallie explained to him that they had no food either but he was welcome to come in and warm himself by the fire. The old man thanked her and came into the kitchen. After he had settled down and was speaking to the boys, Mallie went to the herring barrel.

There were no herring in it, she knew that, but there was some brine. She went to the meal girner and, using a small brush made from the grass that grew near the shore, she swept the corners of the box, the lid and the bottom.

Mallie was surprised at how much she got from the girner, she took it and mixed it with the brine. It was enough that everyone got a small amount in a cup but Mallie had hardly any for herself.

The old man sat by the fire and asked if he could stay with them overnight.

'We have no bed for you but you are welcome to stay by the fire. We have plenty of peats so at least you can be warm,' Mallie replied.

The following morning one of the boys went to the well for a bucket of water and each of them had a drink. The old man took his departure and he thanked the family for their hospitality.

They all said goodbye and the old man walked away. The boys had gone back indoors and Mallie was about to turn in and shut the door when the man turned back and spoke again to Mallie.

'That meal and brine that we had last night, was that really the very last of your food?' he asked. Mallie told him that it was the last and she had no idea what they would have from now on. The old man considered for a time and then said, 'It is a very special person who will share the very last that they have.'

With that he turned and walked away. Inside there was a gloom settling over the house. Mallie hated to see the boys so hungry and they were trying very hard not to complain. The fire burned down low and one of the boys went to the stack for a basketful of peats. At least they could be warm, he thought. When he came back, Mallie stoked up the fire. The peats were quite big and Mallie broke one in two. Something fell from the peat and tinkled on the floor.

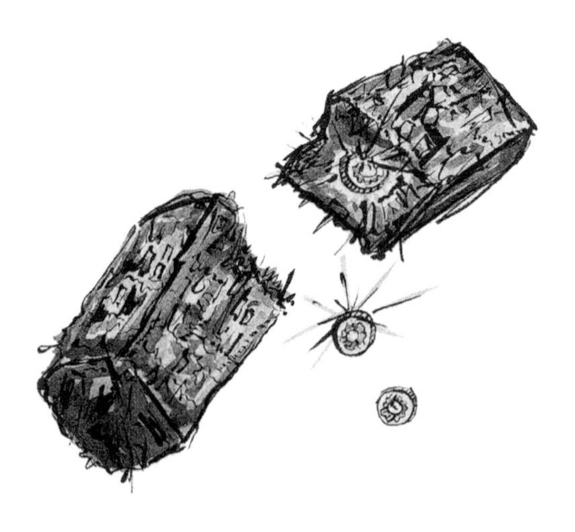

When Mallie picked it up she saw that it was a gold coin. She broke another peat and out came another gold coin. Every peat proved to have a gold coin inside it and Mallie knew that the old man that visited was a trow and this was his way of saying thanks.

There was no more hunger for Mallie and the boys; they could buy anything they wanted. This did not go unnoticed; the old woman who refused to help them was curious to know where Mallie's money came from.

She spied on the family and saw Mallie breaking peats and picking up the coins. The woman waited until after dark and stole peats from Mallie's peat stack. She was not content with a basketful, so she took several and brought them into her kitchen.

However, when she broke a peat no coin appeared. Instead a mouse dropped to the floor and scuttled away looking for a place to hide. She broke open another and another as she looked in vain for gold coins, but all she got was more and more mice.

The mice multiplied like mad and soon the house was overrun with them. They got into her larder and they devoured every morsel of food that she had. In no time she had nothing to eat; the mice had consumed everything.

She endured two days of hunger and misery before she was reduced to begging. She knew that Mallie now had plenty so she came to Mallie's door and was greeted by the same boy that she had turned away from her own door.

The old woman told him that mice had overrun her home, she had no food, she was very hungry and could they please give her something.

'I will give you exactly the same as you gave me when we had nothing,' he told her, and slammed the door in her face.

Mallie asked him who he had been speaking to.

'It was that old woman from next door,' he said. 'She has the cheek to ask us for food and I have not forgotten how she treated me when I asked her for food.'

'Have you forgotten what I told you?' Mallie asked him. 'I told you that we were not like her.'

She opened the door and called the old woman back.

'Come in,' she said. 'Come in and sit by the fire and you can share the food that I am cooking. As long as we have any food you shall never go hungry.'

9

The White Cat

The Shetland Islands are surrounded by some of the richest fishing grounds in the world and fish have been exported from these seas for many hundreds of years. The last years of the nineteenth century and the early twentieth century were the peak times for herring fishing.

Millions of barrels of herring were salted and exported, mainly to Europe. A herring station could be found in every sheltered harbour or voe all around the islands.

Fish curers brought herring from the fishermen and they employed women to gut, salt and pack the herring into barrels. Some of the stations were very large, servicing as many as seven hundred boats and employing people by the thousand.

As well as the women working ashore there were coopers to make and repair barrels, and labourers to carry salt, stack the filled barrels and supply the women with all that they needed.

When the season started, at one station the foreman reported to the fish curer that they had a thief employed. Nothing very big or valuable was taken but it was a steady pilfering and it had to be stamped out.

Almost every day items were reported missing. Coopers lost tools, salt was taken and some wood intended for barrel repairs, as well as hoop iron and nails. The fish curer agreed that this had to be put an end to. He reasoned that if word got out that stealing was tolerated then there would be more and more workers tempted to help themselves.

Catching the thief proved to be easier said than done. It was as if he was always one step ahead and no matter how vigilant they were they could not identify the culprit. The fish curer called a meeting with his foreman and other trusted workers to try and map out a way forward. Many workers had been at the station season after season and they were not suspected. The gutters and packers came from many different places. There were locals but some came from as far away as Scotland and the west coast of Ireland. They were not suspected either.

In the first place the goods taken were not useful to women and besides, the women lived in huts, barrack-type accommodation, they had no privacy and therefore nowhere to conceal anything that they might steal. However, they had ten male workers who were new that season and the meeting agreed that one of them was the thief. But how to catch him?

This was the difficult question that no one had a ready answer to, short of employing security guards, erecting fencing and searching everyone who left the station. This was totally impractical and very costly. After a silence one of the coopers, a local man, said, 'What about asking old Isaac what he thinks?'

Isaac was an old man who lived in a remote place. He had the reputation of being a warlock; some folk called him the Spaeman. In those days there were people who believed in witchcraft and held Isaac in awe. They said, rather darkly, 'That he can do mair dan maet himself.'

In fact, no one seemed to know how Isaac lived – he was a virtual hermit and he had no obvious income. The first reaction of the fish curer was to dismiss this idea. He said that he had no belief in witchcraft and the workforce would laugh at this 'mumbo jumbo'.

In the end, and for want of any better idea, he agreed that the cooper should go and speak to Isaac and hear what he had to say or suggest. The following day the cooper reported back that Isaac claimed that he could unmask the thief but he had to come to the station to do it.

What the cooper did not say was that Isaac had told him that it would be his cat that would sniff out the thief. The cooper thought that if his boss heard this he would veto the whole idea.

Isaac arrived at the station and, sure enough, he had with him this large, snow white cat. Isaac himself looked rather like an Old

Testament prophet. He was old and bent with white hair, a white beard and his clothes were shabby and none too clean.

He made much of walking around the station speaking to everyone in his somewhat shrill voice. He told everyone why he was here and he heavily implied that he was relying on the cat to expose the thief.

The cooper had told him who the suspects were and he had them all gathered together. The fish curer was there too and Isaac ordered the rope and sail store to be cleared. This building had no windows and this was so that none of the cotton nets, ropes and sails was ever exposed to sunlight.

When the door was shut it was pitch dark inside. None of the suspects were allowed to do anything, they had to stand in a group and watch proceedings. When the store was emptied to Isaac's satisfaction he asked for a couch kettle.

Couch kettles were huge iron pots that were used to tan nets and sails, which were all made from cotton and without being couched they quickly rotted because they were always wet.

Couch is derived from tree bark and it comes in powder form and looks like ground coffee. The kettles were placed on the ground or up on a stand, a fire was built around them and the nets or sails were boiled to preserve them.

The kettle that Isaac wanted had to be new out of the fire, filthy and covered in soot and grime. Two men rolled it into the rope store. He wanted it upside down in the middle of the floor and he carefully placed the white cat underneath it so that it was a prisoner there.

He ordered the suspects to enter the store and form a circle around the kettle. Everyone else was to leave the building. Isaac made a drama of closing the door. Now it was pitch, inky black inside.

There was total silence and Isaac allowed the tension to build for a considerable time before ordering the men to take one step forward and to place the palm of their right hand on the kettle.

When he was assured that everyone had done as told, he open the door again and asked them to go outside and form a line along the wall of the building. In contrast to the darkness of the store it was bright sunshine outside.

The cooper, the foreman and the very sceptical fish curer were there to witness the outcome. Isaac ordered them all to raise their right hands, palm outward. Looking along the line of men, their palms were all black from the soot on the kettle. All, that is, except one man – his hand was clean.

Isaac could hardly contain his glee. He jumped around and pointed in triumph.

'There is your thief, he is the one,' he cackled.

When questioned, the man confessed and much of the stolen goods were recovered. The man said that he was frightened to put his hand on the kettle because he believed that the cat would give some signal that would betray him.

The white cat was no more than a red herring, and old Isaac not only had an enhanced reputation but he went home with some money in his pocket given to him by a grateful fish curer.

10

The Raven

Young Tom sat on the crown of the beach with a great many thoughts going through his head. He was waiting to go off fishing with his neighbours, Magnus, James, Andrew and John. Magnus and James were the older men who owned the boat and Andrew and John were younger, nephews by law.

Tom had been warned about what he should not do, and say, in the boat. Magnus especially was very superstitious and there were many taboo words that were never uttered in a boat. For example women were never spoken about and it was bad luck to meet any woman on the way to the beach. If you had to speak about the minister you called him the Upstander or the Beneman. A cat was a *voaler*, a mouse was a *fitelik* and an otter was a *dratsi*.

They were all remnants of the old Norn language spoken in Shetland before the coming of the Scots hundreds of years ago. It was not unknown for the younger men to use some taboo words just for fun, just to annoy the old men.

The men arrived at the beach, the boat was drawn down and the baited lines were stowed on board. Boats were always launched stern first and the men on the oars turned it clockwise, with the sun, or *sungaets* as they put it. To do it any other way would be totally wrong. All the men were expert rowers and soon the boat was speeding smoothly through the calm seas. John was the first one to ruffle Magnus' feathers.

'Did you meet any women on the way to the beach?' he asked Tom. Magnus gave him a hard look.

'I did not,' replied Tom, 'the only thing I saw was an *dratsi* at the burn mouth.'

He realised, too late, that he had made a big mistake. Magnus was clearly annoyed but he said nothing. Andrew then added fuel to the fire.

'It was likely old Inga in one of her guises!'

Inga, as she was known, was an old hag who lived in the village, who Magnus and many others were convinced was a witch. Magnus would go out of his way to avoid her and if he ever saw her close at hand then he was careful to avoid eye contact.

Magnus still never said anything but the look on his face spoke volumes and Andrew and John knew that they had already gone too far so it was wise to keep silent for the time being at least.

After a time, Tom ventured to ask a question.

'Why do we have to go so far away from the land to find fish?'

Magnus explained to him that to find fish on any given day a lot of things had to be taken into consideration, including the season of the year, the state of the tide and the reports from other fishermen about where the fishing was good.

After a long journey out to sea, Magnus told the others to stop rowing. He judged that they were at the right place to set the lines. Fishermen used landmarks and cross bearings to be sure that they were on the right spot.

When the lines with the sinkers and buoys were out of the boat it was time to have a short rest and eat the *faerdimaet*, the food for the trip that they had taken with them. There was also time for the older men to have a smoke of their pipes before Magnus said that they should begin to hail the line.

The first marker was taken into the boat by John and after hauling for a few minutes he felt strong tugging on the line. Soon the white belly of a big fish could be seen down through the clear water. John turned to Andrew.

'Stand by with the huggie staff,' he ordered.

The huggie staff was the gaff, it had a hook on the end for taking big fish into the boat. Andrew used the gaff to good purpose and pulled into the boat a big halibut that weighed as much as eighty pounds.

'Not a bad start,' he commented and this drew another bleak look from Magnus. He had views about what a good start meant. Nonetheless it was the best fish that they had caught all season.

Two large skate followed in quick succession and they were followed by a dogfish that they did not want at all. Andrew put his foot on the dogfish and wrenched it from the hook. With a curse he threw it over the side.

'That's one for old Inga,' he said.

By this time a flock of gulls had arrived in hope of finding some kind of a meal. But Tom noticed another bird with different wing movements coming from the shore and flying low. When it came nearer he was able to identify it. Tom was amazed because he knew that ravens are essentially land birds, they cannot swim or even land on the water. He immediately turned to Magnus and asked, 'How is it that a raven is so far away from the land?'

Magnus growled in reply.

'Never mind what is going on in the sky, pay attention to what is happening in the boat and take the baler and get some of the water out.'

Tom was a little crestfallen at being spoken to so harshly but he knew that the skipper had to be obeyed and he did what he was told. Every second hook on the long line had a dogfish on it and the gulls were screaming in anger at the intrusion of the raven.

Their luck changed again when another large halibut came to the surface. Like lightning the raven swooped and struck at the fish. Magnus and James stopped rowing and gazed in amazement; they had never seen the like before.

'Put a buoy on the line and cut it,' shouted Magnus with urgency.

Andrew was angry. He went to John's side and with a heave and a twist he took the fish into the boat. The raven swooped again and Andrew, with a vicious swipe of the gaff, struck the raven and ripped a great wound in the upper leg of the bird.

It rose with a scream, blood spurting from the tear, and made for the land.

'I will throw away fish for no man,' Andrew said to Magnus. 'But you can cut the line now.'

James said that they should hail the rest of the line because there was not much of it left in the sea. Magnus ignored him; he reached across and cut the line with his knife.

'I will haul the rest of it in my own time,' he said as he took his place with an oar.

The day that Tom had looked forward to so much had turned out very badly and he could not help feeling that it was all his fault. The rowers rowed in silence, every one of them with a grim face.

By the time they got to the beach the light was beginning to fade. All the gear, and the fish, was taken out of the boat and it was hauled up above the high water mark and into the safe place that it was kept in.

John was down at the water's edge, gutting and cleaning the fish, when he noticed a trail of spots on the shingle. When he had finished with the fish he followed the trail and he knew that it was a trail of blood.

'I will go and finish what you started, Andrew,' he said.

When he went over the crown of the beach he uttered such a cry of horror that the others ran to him to see what was wrong. It was old Inga: she was lying on her side, wearing a thin ragged dress – she was dead and already cold. On her leg was a huge gash, from hip to knee, and she had bled to death.

11

The Fiddler and the Cows

One day, a young woman went out to the peat stack to bring in peats for the fire. She was such a long time away that her mother went out to the stack to find out what had become of her.

When she got there she saw no sign of her daughter but the basket to carry the peats in was there. She started to fill the basket thinking that her daughter had gone to speak to some of the neighbours and had lost track of the time.

However, to her horror, when she moved some of the peats she could see that her daughter was buried in the stack. Further investigation showed that she was dead. Why she had died and how she came to be buried in the stack was a mystery that was never solved.

The dead girl was taken home and she was buried in the cemetery in the time-honoured way. Many folk tried to explain her sudden death, but when it came to how she had been buried in the stack, no one had an answer.

She was a favourite daughter and her family grieved for a long time, but they had to get on with their lives as best they could. As always, in cases of this kind, the pain eased somewhat but her mother pondered on the mystery every single day.

A wedding was to take place and every wedding company had to have a fiddler to lead them from the church to the wedding feast and reception. The fiddler would also be expected to play all night, even until morning, for the dancing.

At this time, in Shetland, fiddlers were not plentiful and the fiddler they approached was one who used to live in the village but now resided some distance away. He readily agreed and they invited him to come the day before the wedding so that he was there in plenty of time.

The fiddler set off as agreed but on his way he was stopped by a man that he met on the road. It was no one that he knew but the man spoke to him and asked if he was on his way to play at a wedding.

The fiddler confirmed that he was and the man then said, 'The wedding you are playing at is not until tomorrow night. My wedding is tonight and I want you to play for me and my bride.'

The fiddler wanted to decline and said that he wanted to be sure that he was in good time for the wedding that he had agreed to play for.

'Do not worry,' said the stranger. 'I will make sure that you are in plenty of time and I promise you it will be the best paid night of your life.'

At last the fiddler agreed and when they came to the place where the wedding was to be held the man said to the fiddler, 'I have a word of warning for you. Do not eat or drink anything except what I give you.'

The fiddler thought that this was very strange but he said nothing. He was shown into a large room and he was given a chair to sit on. He tuned his fiddle and he was all ready to play when the bride and bridegroom led in the wedding company.

When he saw the bride he was so shocked that, at first, he could not play a note. He did not know whether she recognised him but he knew her right away. She was the girl who had been found buried in the peat stack.

The fiddler played as best he could, but his mind was so much in turmoil that he knew he was a long way short of his best. After a time the bridegroom came to him and told him that it was time for him to leave and he said that he would escort him back to the place where they had met.

Before they parted, the fiddler was given some money. It was a lot better than nothing but he was slightly disappointed; with the way that the man had spoken earlier he expected far more.

'Use this money to buy a cow,' the man told the fiddler. 'If you do that your byre will flourish with cows, but do not, on any account, tell anyone where you have been or where you got the money to buy the cow.'

The fiddler went on his way and played at the wedding of his friend. He was careful not to say anything about the previous evening. When he got back to his own home he went to a cattle sale and bought a cow as the man suggested.

In time he had a byre full of the best quality beasts in the parish. His cattle were the envy of every farmer, large and small. Even in times when fodder was scarce his cows always looked in prime condition.

Around the island it was talked about but the fiddler never gave anything away. Some farmers' wives made friends with the fiddler's wife in the hope that she would reveal the secret of her husband's success.

Of course she could not tell them because she did not know either. All she knew was that they were a lot better-off now than they used to be. Every time they took an animal to market they got a better price than anyone else.

One winter's night, when the fiddler and his wife were sitting close to the fire, she asked him what it was that he did to make their cattle the best on the island. After some thought he told her the whole story about the wedding, the bride who had been buried and the man who had given him the money; that turned out to be a big mistake. He had disobeyed the bridegroom and his luck changed with a vengeance. The very next day one of his cows died and the day after that another died, and the day after that, and so on until all of his cows had died and his byre was empty.

12

Tommy and the Wicked Witch

Tommy was a young lad who was full of energy, full of mischief and never out of trouble for long. But everyone liked Tommy and the kind of trouble he got into earned him a few scoldings but never more than that.

One person who did not like Tommy, or any children, was old Lucky Minnie. She was an old hag who lived by herself in a cottage near to the burn. But no one liked her very much because she was a witch. She practiced all sorts of cantrips and she was very quick to put a curse on anyone who offended her. If a ewe aborted her lamb or if a fisherman caught no fish or if bad weather ruined any social event then old Lucky Minnie got the blame.

Tommy's mother told him every day not to go anywhere near Lucky Minnie's cottage. If she found a child near her home she accused them of snooping and she would give them a beating and send them home crying.

The folk of the village were afraid to challenge old Lucky Minnie, afraid of what she would do to get revenge. So they kept out of her way and had as little to do with her as possible. No one knew how she made her living but she always seemed to have plenty.

Tommy was very discontented because he had been indoors for several days. It had never stopped raining and the wind was fierce too. Every morning, as soon as he opened his eyes, he jumped out of bed and ran to the window to see if the weather was any better.

When the weather was better Tommy could not wait to get outdoors and go on some sort of an adventure. He would have set off without any breakfast but his mother made him sit at the table and eat his porridge.

When he got outside it was the most beautiful morning. The sun was shining, there was no wind, the birds were all singing and Tommy could hear the noise of the sea, it had not settled down after all the storms.

Tommy had been warned, as usual, not to go anywhere near old Lucky Minnie's house but it was like a magnet to Tommy. He marvelled at the size of the burn, he had never seen it so full and in places it looked like overflowing.

He approached Lucky Minnie's place with a degree of caution; if she was outside he knew that he would be lucky to get away with no more than a telling off. The door of her cottage was wide open and he could see into her kitchen.

Lucky Minnie was spring cleaning and she had all her best dishes laid out to wash and polish. Tommy had never seen so many beautiful dishes before. There were cups, saucers, plates of different sizes, there were serving dishes, jugs, sugar bowls and teapots and much more. They all had bright colourful patterns and pictures of fruit painted on them. Tommy watched, wide eyed, as old Lucky Minnie very carefully rinsed them all and stacked them up to dry. All the while Tommy was getting bolder and ventured nearer and nearer to the door.

All of a sudden old Lucky Minnie looked over her shoulder and saw Tommy. He could not believe how quick she moved. With a scream of rage she darted out the door and caught Tommy by the scruff of the neck and dragged him inside.

'You were spying on me you little brat and I am going to teach you a lesson that you will never forget!' she roared.

She never released her hold on Tommy but she opened a cupboard door and brought out a thick canvas bag; a bag like the one that sailors used to carry their clothes in. She pulled the top wide open and put Tommy inside.

Tightening the drawstring on the bag, she was confident that Tommy was secured, a prisoner in the bag. But just to make sure, she hung it on a peg in the wall. She told Tommy that he could hang there until she came back.

'I have gone to the barn,' she told him. 'I am going to fetch a flail staff and I will thresh you within an inch of your life.'

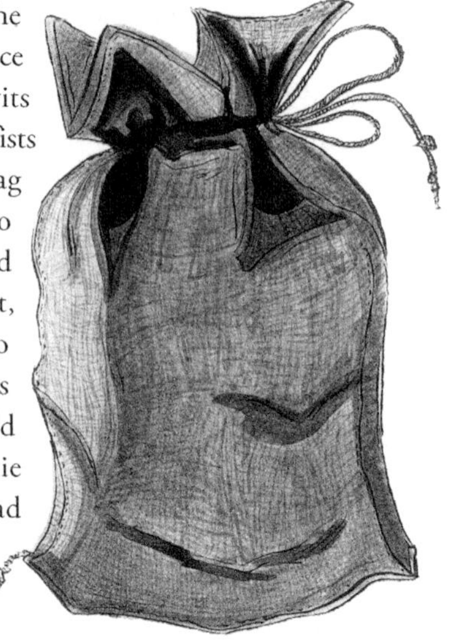

Being captured and stuffed into the bag was a most unpleasant experience for Tommy but he had kept his wits about him and had raised both his fists and put them at the top of the bag before Lucky Minnie had tied it. So Lucky Minnie, who thought she had tied the bag tight, had, in fact, not, leaving Tommy with some room to move. Nonetheless, Tommy was fearful; one of his friends had told him of the time that Lucky Minnie put him in the same bag and had threshed him with the flail. When she finally let him go he was all black and blue and at first he thought that maybe he had broken bones.

Tommy knew that she hated him more than any other child on the island – she would make him suffer. His only hope was to get out of the bag and escape while she was at the barn. He lost no time in getting his hand out where the drawstring was slack and his deft fingers untied the knots and opened the bag.

Being slim and very nimble he quickly climbed out and dropped down to the floor. His first thought was to put as much distance as possible between himself and the old witch.

Just as he was about to leave the house he had a really wicked idea. It was highly dangerous but worth taking a risk – the idea was so good! There was no time to ponder, Lucky Minnie could come back at any time.

As quickly as he could Tommy scooped up all of the beautiful dishes and put them into the bag and hung it back on the wall. Now was definitely the time to clear out but his curiosity got the better of him, he simply had to see if his idea worked.

No sooner had he hidden himself behind a big rock than old Lucky Minnie appeared carrying the flail. She was muttering and cursing Tommy and gloating about the hammering that she was about to give him. Her fury was ugly to see and Tommy was so grateful to have escaped.

Lucky Minnie was swinging the flail as she went in the door and she began to lambaste the bag with all her strength. She had hit it four or five times before she realised that the sounds coming out of the bags were not howls of pain from Tommy. It was altogether a different sound: it was the sound of fine china being smashed to smithereens. When she looked in the bags not one item of her fine crockery remained whole. When she heard Tommy laughing she was beside herself with fury.

'I'll kill you, I'll kill you!' she screamed as she went to find the boy.

Tommy took to his heels and ran faster than he had ever run before but he had seen how fast Lucky Minnie could run and was not sure that he could outpace her. But his fertile brain had another idea: he would cross the burn and that might slow her down.

The burn was so big and wide that this was risky, but well worth it to avoid the old witch's clutches. Tommy never hesitated; he jumped from the bank onto a stone in the middle of the burn and from there to the far side.

Lucky Minnie followed him but she was not so careful where she put her feet. She jumped onto a slippery stone, slid off and fell into the raging water. Tommy watched as she was carried away by the force of the burn and into the sea.

Lucky Minnie was never seen again and no one was sorry to see the last of her. For once Tommy got no scolding for going to her house; in fact, he was something of a folk hero.

13

THE BUTTER STONE

Christina was a young woman who was about to be married. Like every young bride-to-be she was very much looking forward to the big day. She was excited and her head was full of a thousand things that had to be in place for the big event.

Christina was a religious girl and popular in the community. Her husband-to-be lived a distance away and after the wedding Christina was to leave her home village to live with her man.

Old Maggie was a neighbour of Christina's but she was house-bound and she sent word that she wanted to talk to Christina before she left. Maggie had always been kind to her so she readily went to see the old lady.

Maggie thanked her for coming and said that she was sorry that Christina was leaving the village and that she would not see so much of her in the future.

'I wish that I had something really nice to give you for a wedding present but I don't,' said the old lady. 'But I will give you this and you may find it useful.'

Maggie rose from her chair and, holding onto furniture, she made her way slowly and painfully to the dresser. She opened a drawer and took out an old sock. After she had resumed her chair by the fire she put her hand into the sock and drew out something wrapped in a piece of cloth.

From the cloth she held up two small stones, one yellow and one white.

'The yellow one is a butter stone and the white one is a milk stone,' she explained.

Christina had no idea what she meant so she waited for more information. After a pause Maggie continued, 'Those stones have served me well but my day is done now and I have no further use for them so I want to pass them on to you. They have been especially enchanted by the trows.'

'What would I do with them?' asked Christina.

Maggie held up the white stone.

'If you are ever in need of milk, if your cow has little milk to give, then you use this stone. Heat the stone, dip it in water and then, using the tongs, turn it three times with the sun and three times against the sun. Point the tongs at whatever house in the parish you want the milk from, some house that has a good milking cow, and say this rhyme: Tak fae intil aa's teen, enough ta blaw dee fae da bane.* When you want the spell broken you turn the tongs back to your own house. I did the same with the yellow stone if I wanted a good bit of butter from someone else's cow.'

Maggie wrapped the stones again in the cloth and put them back in the sock and offered them to Christina. Christina was unsure whether she should take them or not but she did not want to offend old Maggie; she did not believe that it was any more than an old wife's tale and she never saw herself putting them to the test.

She never told anyone of her conversation with Maggie, not even her husband. The wedding took place and Christina settled down to married life. Her husband was a crofter and a fisherman, as were most of their neighbours.

When the men were at sea, the work on the land and the looking after of animals was the work of the women. One day, years later, when she was home alone, Christina set about churning. The milking cow gave little milk and the quality of the milk was not good either and Christina felt that her efforts would yield nothing.

She had never given a thought to the stones that she had got from old Maggie but they came to her mind now. Maggie herself had passed away but Christina still kept the stones in a safe place.

*Take everything until it is all taken, enough that will make you fat.

I wonder if they work? she thought. Only one way to find out, she said to herself.

She took the stones from the sock and the cloth and heated the yellow stone in the fire, dipped it in water and turned it, with the tongs, three times with the sun and three times against the sun.

'Tak fae intil aa's teen, mite blaw dee fae da bane.' She chanted the rhyme and pointed the tongs at a house on the other side of the valley. The woman who lived there was always bragging about how good her cow was and how the cow gave far more milk than she could ever use.

Christina's churn was the upright sort, rather like a slim barrel, and from the moment that she put the staff into the milk she knew that something out of the ordinary was happening. The milk was frothing up the colour of rich cream; she had never seen the like before.

She was afraid that if any of the neighbours came in she was going to have to explain the amazing results of the churning. The churn was heavy but she managed to carry it into another room where it would not be seen.

But the butter kept coming – in all her life she had never seen so much butter from one churning. After she had taken all the butter from the churn she was careful to break the spell by turning the tong the opposite way around.

Two days later the storm broke. The woman who owned the good cow was furious; she knew full well that someone had stolen the profit from her cow but she did not know who. She shouted for all to hear her that she was going to the minister and the kirk session and the person responsible would be severely punished.

She said that she knew who the person was but strangely enough she did not blame Christina. She said that Christina was too nice a person to do anything so evil and wicked.

Christina saw it as a lesson learned. She knew that she had got away with doing something that she should never have done. She waited until one quiet day when no one was around and, taking a spade, she dug a deep hole in the yard and buried the stones. No doubt they are there yet.

14

Witch Against Witch

In poor rural communities folk worked together and helped each other and often the crofting and peat harvesting was done in a co-operative manner. However, that did not mean that there was no rivalry or ill feeling among individuals.

Sometimes old women living close together quarrelled; seldom did this come out into the open but there could be animosity. Sometimes those women fancied themselves as witches and they would seek to put spells and curses on each other.

Two women who were neighbours both had the reputation that they 'could do more than maet themselves', the local way of saying that they could make things happen – that they were witches.

One of the women, Ursella, had a cow that was about to have a calf. She also had a granddaughter who was still a child. The other woman, Naunie, invited the little girl into her house and gave her a sweet biscuit.

'I want you to tell me,' said Naunie to the little girl, 'when the cow has calved and when your granny sits down to take the first milk from her, but you must not tell anyone else.'

Being so young and innocent the girl did not know that her granny was included among those who must not be told. She came home and announced that 'Naunie wants to know when you are ready to milk the cow'.

'Oh she does, does she!' exclaimed Ursella. 'Maybe I can give her a surprise.'

After a few days the cow did have her calf and everything was just the way it should be. The first milk from a cow newly calved is especially rich and many folk saw it as a delicacy. It could be boiled or put in a dish and baked in the oven. Either way it looked rather like scrambled eggs.

Ursella called over the little girl. 'Away and tell Naunie that I am about to milk the cow for the first time.'

She did as she was told and Naunie thanked her and gave her another biscuit. The girl sat down and watched Naunie fetch a bucket and a length of rope. In those days every house had lines stretching across the room as near to the fire as possible.

They were known as raeps and they were used to hang salted fish and meat to be dried among the peat smoke. Naunie put one end of her rope over the raep and allowed both ends to hang just above the bucket.

She drew in a stool and took the rope's ends, one in each hand, and began to tug downwards on them as if she were milking a cow. But she got no milk; what she did get was cows' dung that fell into her bucket with every tug on the rope.

With a howl of rage Naunie got up from the stool and she threw the rope and the bucket out the door. She ordered the little girl out of the house and told her never to come back. When she got home she told her granny what had happened and Ursella found it very funny.

'That old Naunie has found out that she is not the only one who has a bit of magic and it will be a long time before she tries to steal the profit from my cow.'

In those days there was no electricity and there was no way of preserving meat or fish except by salting. True it could be smoked but that never lasted all winter and that was what was needed.

It was the practice, therefore, in a township, that the killing of animals was staggered. When a family slaughtered, say, a pig, they would give a piece of the fresh meat to each of the neighbours and the compliment was returned when their beasts were killed.

With food, and especially fresh meat, being so scarce, a balance had to be struck in regard to what was given away. Too small a cut or a poor quality cut could not be offered, that was a matter of pride.

It seemed that it was largely the women who gave and received the gifts. On one occasion one woman gave to another a prime cut.

The two women did not like each other so it was doubly important to put on a brave showing.

However, when a gift of meat was returned it was a poor scrappy cut, poor quality and not that much of it. The receiver was furious; she had been at pains to give a generous, quality cut and this was near rubbish that she had got in return. So angry was she that she put a curse on the other woman that went like this: 'May Guid grant that she skitters until her erse can't mark white paper!'

15

A Spanish Ship Visits

The island of Papa Stour lies off the west coast of the Shetland Mainland. Like so many of the place names of Shetland it was named by the Vikings. *Papa*, or papil, means priests and *Stour* means big, so it was the big island of priests.

One morning, when the folk of Papa Stour got up and looked out they saw a strange ship anchored in the bay. It was not unusual for a ship to call; it could be that they needed fresh water or it might be that they sought shelter.

At that particular time shelter was not an issue. The wind was blowing offshore and the ship was in perfect shelter but it was no more than a gentle breeze and there were no signs of worse weather to come.

This ship was black and sleek; she had a sinister appearance and she flew no flag and there was no hint as to her nationality. Neither were there any signs of lowering a boat to come ashore and make contact with the Papa Stour folk.

The strange ship had an air of menace that prevented any of the locals approaching her. In fact, everyone hoped that she would raise her anchor and go. The day went on and nothing at all happened but there was a feeling of unease on the whole island.

Two men were working on a boat at the shore. It was evening and the daylight was beginning to fade when they were aware of something happening. They heard splashing in the sea and, at first, they thought it was a seal.

It was, in fact, a man swimming for the shore as if his life depended on it. He was about the last of it when the boat builders helped him from the sea. He was half drowned and so out of breath that he could not speak.

After sitting down on a rock for a time he recovered sufficiently to tell them that he was an Englishman who had been held prisoner on the ship. He had managed to break free and jump over the side and escape.

He further told them that the ship was Spanish but it was a pirate ship and the crew fully intended to land on Papa Stour tomorrow and ransack the island. This was alarming news indeed.

The two men took the refugee home with them and they lost no time in spreading the news of the imminent danger. The senior men on the island held a council of war and they tried to decide how best they could defend themselves.

They were a peace-loving people and they were fully aware that they had no defence against an viscious armed attack. They discussed many different ideas and none of them gave an effective answer.

They discussed the possibility of hiding all their valuables in the many caves around the coast but the Englishman told them that this would never work. The pirates were ruthless and cruel, they might well use torture to extract information. There was also the possibility that they would take the youngest and strongest prisoner to sell into the slave trade. No matter how it was viewed it was a bleak outlook. One man spoke with hesitation and little confidence because he did not expect that his suggestion would find favour.

'Maybe we should ask Minna Baabie for help,' he said.

Silence fell in the room. Minna Baabie was a powerful witch who all were frightened of and everyone was at pains to avoid any contact with her. After some time, one of the elders spoke up, 'I don't like the idea of having anything to do with Minna Baabie. She is evil and she despises everything that I stand for, but we are faced with evil and maybe the use of evil is the best solution.'

The elder and another man went to see Minna Baabie. She was an ugly old hag and she lived in a small cottage that was little more than a hovel. The men told her about the Spanish ship and the danger that it posed to the island and they asked her for help.

Minna Baabie was very slow to answer. She pondered for a long time but eventually she agreed to help them.

'I will help you,' she said, 'if you will promise to give me the neck of the fattest ox from Fugla Skerry when the killing time comes.'

Fugla Skerry was a green holm with rich grass that produced fat, high-quality animals. The men who had animals on Fugla Skerry readily agreed to the witch's terms and they asked what else she needed to complete her task.

She advised the fishermen to secure their boats and houses that they used for curing fish. She said that they should prepare for winter weather. She also said that she needed to go to a two-storey house, a house with a stairs.

Minna Baabie used a staff and she walked with difficulty but she hobbled along the path to Haa of Kirkhouse. When she arrived she went straight to the stairs and slowly, painfully, began to ascend.

After only two steps there was a murmur of wind that was heard by those around her. There was also a noise from the sea.

Minna Baabie mounted another two steps and the noise of the wind and the sea increased markedly.

By the time that she got to the top of the stairs the wind was hurricane force and the sea was so rough that when a wave broke on the shore the spray covered the whole island. This violent storm lasted as long as she was at the top of the stairs.

As she descended the stairs the wind gradually eased and by the time that she was at the bottom it was no more than the gentle breeze that it had been all day. The following morning, when the daylight came in, there was no sign of the Spanish ship. It had disappeared and it was never again seen by the folk of Papa Stour.

16

The Fairy's Wine Well

The deep valley of Arisdale is in South Yell. It is surrounded on high hills either side and has a wide burn that runs into the sea at Hamnavoe. Near the top of one of those hills is a well. Its whereabouts is not known now but it was said to have magic properties. The well had been built in, with stone walls and a stone slab covered the top. The overflow from the spring could be heard running underground.

Whenever a baby was born in the area someone would go and visit the well. If they could hear music coming from it then they knew that mother and baby was fine and that state of affairs would continue. However, if no music was heard then they knew that something bad was going to happen.

The water from the well was very special indeed. It did not matter how warm a summer day was, the water was always ice cold and refreshing. It did not matter how much rain fell, the water in the well never became discoloured. It was always crystal clear and had a taste like no other water. Some said that the fairies made it into wine and some declared that it was so delicious that it was wine already. Sick people drank it, as it was reckoned to have healing properties.

Above all it was believed it could cure insanity, but not everyone thought this to be true. In a neighbouring parish there was a man who had become insane. The poor man did not have a rational thought and he had become so difficult to care for that his family was at their wits' end to know what to do.

His wife heard about the fairy's well so she sent her grown-up son to go to it and bring back a bucket of water. The son had no belief in the powers of the water so he went to another well, a well that was much nearer and not up such a steep hill!

He brought it back to the house and offered a jug of water to his father. He tasted the water and then threw the jug with great force against the wall. It shattered into fragments and the water was spilt. This was typical of his behaviour yet he said with vehemence, 'This is not the right water!'

Coming from him this was a very surprising statement. His wife saw the guilty look on the son's face and asked if the water truly was from the fairy's well.

'It's a lot of rubbish,' he said. 'The water there is no different from any other water and it's a waste of time climbing that steep hill.'

His mother was adamant and the very next day she set out with a bucket and brought back a bucket of the water. She had tasted it at the well and found it most refreshing after the long walk and the steep climb.

The sick man drank it greedily and when it was finished he wanted more. The son went the next day and this time he did not seek to cheat. As every day went past the father got better, and after a week or so he was perfectly normal, as sane as anyone else in the parish.

He was a religious man and he began to attend church once more and every Sunday he went to the fairy's well and got water for himself. He remained sane and sensible for the rest of his life and died at the age of eighty-six.

17

The Gloup Disaster

Fishing from sixtreens was a dangerous business but it was the preferred method of fishing during the eighteenth and nineteenth centuries in Shetland. One of the biggest fishing ports, or stations as they were known, was in Gloup, North Yell.

The most desired fish were ling, cod and tusk. (Mackerel were seldom eaten, being considered inferior and not fit for anything but bait.) The fishing was with long lines. Lines were anything up to half a mile long and would have five hundred hooks. The fish, when landed, were split and salted before being dried in the sun. The main markets were Catholic countries that did not eat meat on Fridays.

As a rule, boats would leave the shore in the early morning. If the wind was favourable they would sail, otherwise they would row. It could take as long as twelve hours to reach the fishing grounds anything up to forty miles away.

The lines were then set and the men might have a short break before hailing started. It was all done by hand and could be back-breaking work, but with the lines, and the catch, on board they would set off back to the shore.

Again it was a case of sailing if they could and rowing if they had to but all going well they would reach their home station in the late afternoon or early evening. This was thirty-six hours of very hard work with little or no sleep and no hot food.

They would have some food with them and they usually had an iron kettle of fire to keep them warm. Those men were noted for having strong stomachs and for some a favourite snack was a liver head. They would gut a fish and cut off the head. They would then

stuff the fish's liver into the head and put it in the fire kettle until the liver melted, before eating it.

The fishermen themselves had nothing to do with the fish after they were landed. The fishing boat and the lines all belonged to the landowners and the merchants; fishermen had to sell their catches to them at whatever price they decided to pay.

Fishermen and their families were really poor and those who were too old to fish, or women who were widowed or single, were even worse off. Sometimes the filletters deliberately did a poor job, leaving a quantity of fish on the bones, which once boiled could make a meal for a poor person.

The serfdom imposed by the landowners and merchants was bad enough but this type of fishing was also extremely dangerous. All too often a man, or even a boat and crew, were lost and there was no welfare service to help widows and orphans.

The worst fishing disaster to hit the island of Yell occurred on the morning of 21 July 1881. From the station of Nedertoon in Gloup, six boats and thirty-six men were lost. For a small community this was a devastating blow.

Almost every household in North Yell was affected and even a hundred years later it was spoken about in low voices and referred to as simply 'the bad morning'. There have been many things said about the lead up to, and the aftermath of, the disaster.

One week before, a fisherman died at the station. He died in the lodge, the bothy-type accommodation that the fishermen used. In the days when there was no motor transport it was easier for some men to stay in the lodge than walk many miles to get home.

As a mark of respect, no fishing was done until after the funeral. The funeral took place on 19 July, and the following day fishing was to start again. Fishermen were desperate to get back to work; they could ill afford to lose fishing time, funeral or no funeral.

Some of the older men did not like the look of the weather, the morning was somewhat eerie; there was no wind at all, it was muggy, close, with a very low cloud base and it was raining heavily, straight down from the top of the sky. It all added up to the likelihood of bad weather to come.

Pressurised by the need to fish, many of the older men went off against their better judgement. The first part of the trip went well, with nothing out of the ordinary happening, but late in the evening the wind began to rise, and it was soon storm force. The seas got up too. The fishermen franticly hauled in the lines, not caring whether they had fish or not. As soon as possible they made for the shore with the wind behind them. They used the sail but had it close reefed.

It has been said since that a wiser course of action would have been to stay with the lines, use them as a sea anchor and ride out the storm at sea. As far as is known all the boats survived until they came close to the land.

There is little darkness in a Shetland summer night but the morning of 21 July was an exception. Driving before such violent winds accurate navigation was near impossible and land was never sighted until they were dangerously close to it.

Needless to say they could not simply land just anywhere, it had to be a safe place with a beach. It was in turning away from cliffs and rugged shores that the boats were lost. When daylight dawned, families gathered at Nedertoon to meet the survivors but sadly there were not many.

In those days communications were slow and there was hope that maybe some boats had come ashore on neighbouring islands or perhaps missed the island altogether. In the days that followed hope was abandoned and bodies were found in places far away from the home station.

The plight of the widows and orphans was dire. Not only had the breadwinner been lost but the lairds and the merchants who owned the boats and the lines demanded compensation for their loss.

This was a pointless exercise because they had nothing to pay with. In some cases that did not stop the heartless lairds evicting some of the widows and confiscating the few possessions that they owned.

In time, folk could look back and think about the disaster and they discussed incidents that perhaps foretold the tragedy to come and they looked back to the funeral that took place on that day.

Women never went to funerals but a few of them watched the funeral procession and they noticed a low black cloud that followed the men carrying the coffin. The minister who conducted the funeral service was seen to behave oddly in the graveyard.

He was very old but he went out of his way to shake the hands of several men present and said that maybe they would not see him again. They all assumed that he was referring to his own fragility, saying, in other words, that he did not have long to live.

Other men he ignored and when folk compared notes they realised that the ones who had the handshakes were the ones going to be lost in the disaster. One woman recalled the experience she had a few days before the disaster.

She washed a shirt belonging to her husband and hung it out to dry along with other clothes. When she went out to see if it was dry she saw three drops of blood on it. She took it in and washed it again.

She thought that perhaps the blood had come from a wounded bird. But the three spots reappeared and no matter how often she washed the shirt the blood reappeared. Her husband was one of those lost that bad morning.

One hundred years later, in 1981, a permanent memorial to the fishermen was unveiled. It stands on the side of the lea overlooking Gloup Voe and Nedertoon. It is a beautiful stone sculpture and takes the form of a young mother, with a baby in her arms, looking out to sea for any sign of her husband returning.

18

Flokki of the Ravens

The biggest lake in the middle of the Shetland Mainland is the Loch of Girlsta. Not only does it have a large surface area but it is also deep, around twenty-two metres. In the middle of it there is an island and this is the last resting place of a Viking girl, Geirhilda.

Her father was a well-known Viking, Flokki Vilgerdarson, Ramna Flokki or Flokki of the Ravens. He was a warrior, a trader and an explorer. He came to the area because he wanted to capture ravens. Seafarers like Flokki used ravens as a navigational aid. Ravens are land birds, they cannot swim or even sit on the water so they always seek land.

Flokki's wife had died and that was why he had taken Geirhilda with him on this expedition. Flokki had heard rumours that there was a big land away to the north and away to the west and he wanted to find it.

However, a great sorrow came to Flokki when Geirhilda drowned in the loch. She was a beautiful teenager and she had recently come into conflict with her father because he strongly disapproved of the young man that she had taken as a lover.

Flokki had forbidden her to see this man but she sneaked out at night; the young lovers had arranged to meet in secret. Geirhilda had probably lost her way in the dark and stumbled into the loch. Her body was found near the shore the following morning and her father had her buried on the island.

Flokki's grief was terrible to see – Geirhilda was all he had left – but he was a Viking and he had seen death in plenty before. Indeed, he had killed many men in his time. After a while he was ready to get on with his life and his men were successful in capturing three ravens.

They set sail for the Faroe Islands and then continued on in roughly a north-westerly direction. After several days at sea Flokki released a raven and, after a few circles around the longship, it headed back the way they had come.

This told Flokki that they were still within the raven's range of Faroe. After another few days at sea Flokki released a second raven and this one never left the proximity of the longship. It circled until it was exhausted and then came back to the ship.

This told Flokki that they were a very long way away from land. After another four days Flokki released the third raven and this time the bird flew onwards in more or less the same direction as they were steering.

Flokki followed it and the next day, late in the afternoon, they sighted land. And so it was that Ramna Flokki became one of the very first people to set foot on Iceland. Flokki was disappointed, he hoped for a more promising new land.

It was late in the season and already it was cold and he gave it the name – Iceland. The death of Geirhilda had badly upset Flokki's plans. If this had not happened he would have reached Iceland while there was some summer left.

But as it was it was far too late in the year to make the return journey to Norway and Flokki had no alternative but spend the winter in Iceland. It proved to be an extremely hard winter even by Icelandic standards and some of Flokki's men died of cold and hunger. Flokki cursed the day that he decided to seek this awful place.

The cold was intense, the ground was as hard as rock, the rivers and lakes were all frozen and even the sea had ice in it. Food was very hard to find and the winter seemed to have no end.

Eventually the days became longer and a thaw replaced the frost and Flokki and his men discovered rivers teeming with fish; they discovered the fertile valleys enhanced by the geothermal heat and Iceland was transformed from a desolate wasteland to a land of plenty.

Even so, Flokki set off back home to Norway. However, images of Iceland remained in his head. With his wife and Geirhilda both dead there was nothing to keep him in Norway so he decided to return to Iceland.

Now he knew how to survive a hard winter and he lived in Iceland for all the rest of his days, one of the early settlers there.

Visitors to the wonderful Pearl Museum in Reykjavik can see a replica longship with a waxwork of Flokki standing up about to release a raven. They give the year as 879.

19

THE COW KILLERS

The island of Yell in Shetland is seventeen miles long and six miles wide. The population lives mostly around the coastal areas and the interior is largely empty. Before the days of good roads and motor transport most people walked to the places they wanted to go to.

Magnus lived in Gossabrough, a hamlet near the southeast corner of the island and he set out to visit his sister who lived in Vigo, on the extreme northwest corner of Yell.

For Magnus the only way to go was through the hills, a trackless wilderness crossing the island, and then to walk up the west coast. Given the rough ground, the hills and the difficult walking conditions he expected his journey to take most of the day.

He set off in the morning; it was a fine day weatherwise and he took with him some *faerdamaet*, food to sustain him on his long walk. He took two ribs of cooked salt pork and several big, round oatcakes called brünnies. He had no need to take water, in an entirely clean environment he could drink from any stream that he crossed.

His direction was north-westerly and with the sun on his back he enjoyed the walk, seeing the wildlife and listening to the birds singing. Several times he sat down on hilltops to rest and partake in some of his store of food.

He passed the narrow middle of the island and headed for the west side. He was reaching the coast at a place called Markamoot and this is the most isolated part of the island, a place where no one lived or had ever lived.

It came as a big surprise then when he heard human voices and they came from underneath the cliffs. Getting a little nearer he saw that the sea, close to the shore, was red and this made Magnus very nervous indeed.

With extra caution he looked down from the clifftop into the geo below and he was horrified at what he saw. There were four men and two women and they were butchering a cow.

Magnus knew that not only was he looking at a crime scene but at a very serious crime being committed. Sheep thieves were severely punished; a death sentence was not unknown. To be out of sight he hurriedly stepped back but as he did so he dislodged a small stone that rattled down the sloping cliff face.

Immediately the folk below knew that their crime had been observed and the youngest of the men, as quick as sheepdog, ran up to the top and chased Magnus. Magnus tried to run away but he had no chance; after a few yards this young man wrapped his arms around Magnus and in one hand he carried a knife.

Magnus was marched back and down into the geo at knifepoint and the cow thieves discussed how they would deal with him.

'Mütil him, mütil him,' demanded one of the women, meaning that his throat should be cut. The oldest of the men said a very firm 'no' to this but he knew that they were in a desperate fix. There would be a heavy price to pay if they were found out.

Magnus pleaded for his life; he told them that he did not know them and, for all that he knew, it might be their own cow that they had killed. This made little impression and the two women were still in favour of murdering him – they argued that this was the only way of keeping him quiet.

In the end they knew that they could not murder him in cold blood. They decided to free him, but before they did they made him lie on his knees, put his hands together and swear a solemn oath. He had to swear by his Maker that he would never tell any human being what he had seen that day.

Once clear of the thieves he made what speed he could to get as far away from them as possible. Tiredness got the better of him and he sat down to rest and think things through. He was relieved to escape with his life but he was also angry that those thieves might get off scot-free.

He did not know what course of action to take. On the one hand he wanted those murderous thieves to face justice, but on the other hand he had sworn an oath of silence and that he could not abandon lightly. Gradually he formed a plan that might serve to square the circle.

When he arrived at Vigon he was greeted with great affection by his sister Maggie and her husband Jeemie. No member of the household gave him a warmer welcome than the old sheepdog, Tippy. Magnus knew Tippy of old and he was jumping up and trying to lick Magnus's hands and face.

Maggie had a delicious meal of fresh fish and potatoes all but ready to put on the table. After his long walk Magnus was hungry and the good food and the catching up with news helped to mellow the memory of the ordeal experienced at Markamoot.

The house of Vigon was small and Maggie said that she and Jeemie would sleep in the box bed in the kitchen and Magnus was to sleep in the ben bed. After such a stressful day, Magnus said that he wanted an early bed so he went through to prepare and Tippy, as always, followed him.

Magnus sat on the edge of the bed and Tippy laid his head on Magnus's knee to be stroked. As Magnus petted the dog he told Tippy about his journey from Gossabrough to Vigon. All the doors were open and Magnus knew that Maggie and Jeemie could hear every word that he said.

He told Tippy all about what he saw at Markamoot and how the thieves had threatened to kill him. This was how news of the thieves and their crime was made known, and Magnus felt that he had not broken his oath because he had not told another human being – it was the dog that he told.

20

The Marriage of Hughie Brown

The island of Unst is the most northerly of all the Shetland Islands. It is separated from Yell by the narrow and very tidal Bluemull Sound. People from the two islands have a close relationship and there are a great many inter-island marriages.

Yell man Hughie Brown was betrothed to Mina Robertson from north Unst. They had been courting for some time and Hughie went to Unst every weekend, where Mina and he would attend social events in Unst and Yell.

In those days they did not talk about being engaged and it was highly unusual for any rings to be exchanged at this stage. The term used was 'on the heads of marriage' and this meant that a marriage would certainly take place; it was just a question of when and where.

Hughie and Mina's wedding date was set for the autumn. It was a popular time for marriage for a number of reasons. It was a time when all the crops were in, people were less busy, men had been paid for animals sold and fishermen had had their settlements for the season. It was also the season when sheep, lambs and geese were being slaughtered, providing a wedding feast.

Like every other young bride-to-be, Mina was very excited as the big day approached. She and her mother had been working on her wedding dress, planning and preparing. There was much to do: as well as the food to prepare, there were the helpers to ask and musicians had to be given their 'fiddler's bid'.

A fiddler's bid was so called because sometimes one might be invited to a wedding, not because they were wanted there as a friend or relation, but because they could play the fiddle and would, therefore, be useful at the wedding dance.

It was less than two weeks until the wedding day and Mina was thinking about the contract night. This was the night when the marriage agreement was nailed down once and for all and it followed a set routine.

The bridegroom and his best man would go to the session clerk – he was an official of the church – to collect the proclamation, the marriage banns. The banns were delivered to the minister and he would read them out in church on the Sunday before the marriage.

The bridegroom and the best man would then go to the bride's house and the groom would have a bottle with him, a bottle of spirits. This was known as the spöring bottle. He would ask for a glass and he would fill it and offer it to his father-in-law-to-be.

In doing so he was pledging himself to the family and promising to be a dutiful husband. In accepting the drink the man of the house was accepting the groom as his son and as full member of the family.

The weekend came and Hughie never appeared. The Robertson household could not understand, he had never missed a weekend since he and Mina got together. Without telephones communications were slow but, at the very least they expected some word of explanation from Hughie.

A letter arrived on Tuesday addressed to Mina and it was with a sinking heart that she broke the seal and opened it. It was from Hughie. It was brief, but it said quite starkly that he had changed his mind. He did not want to marry Mina and the wedding was off.

Mina was devastated by this news. She was inconsolable and she went to bed, sobbing her heart out and refused to get up either that day or any other day. So broken-hearted was she that she was in bed until it ran into years. She vowed never to trust another man and she was never married.

What Hughie did not tell Mina was that he had found another girl that he loved more than Mina. She was Beena Donaldson and after an interval they were married and settled down in a cottage in Yell near to the shores of Bluemull Sound and enjoyed a happy marriage and raised a family.

Hughie was typical in many ways. He made an income from fishing, he owned a sixtreen. He also had a croft, a smallholding, and while they were poor they had enough to live on.

With few roads on the island anything heavy had to be transported by sea and sometimes Hughie was ask to shift cargo with his sixtreen. He was asked to take two tons of roofing slates from Cullivoe, in the north of the island, to Mid Yell where they were wanted for a large new house under construction.

He got two of his neighbours, brothers John and Robert Sinclair, to be his crew and help load and unload the slates. Slates were never a popular cargo to carry. They had to be stowed very carefully because they were notoriously liable to slide, and with a boat under sail this posed a very real danger.

They set sail from Cullivoe with almost ideal weather conditions; the sea was smooth and the wind was a fresh breeze from the northwest. There was a strong south tide running at around six knots so progress was rapid. However, about a mile and a half into the journey the conditions changed.

The wind became stronger and more uneven. On the landward side was the village of Gutcher and on the seaward side was the uninhabited island of Lingey. Here the tides are distorted by the shape of the land and an eddy of back tide, near the shore, runs in the opposite direction to the main stream.

This causes confusion in the sea – any tides running in the face of the wind makes what fishermen call tide lumps. Beena saw the sixtreen and went outside to wave to Hughie; they were so close that they were almost within shouting distance.

Beena was horrified to see a very strong squall hit the square sail of the sixtreen. There was a loud grinding, grating noise as all the slates slid to the lee side. Combined with the wind this caused the boat to list, the gunwale dipped into the water and the boat filled within seconds.

With the dead weight of the stone slates, it sank in the blink of an eye. The men had no chance; they wore no life jackets and none of them could swim. To see her husband lost before her very eyes was a severe blow to Beena; she could never imagine that such a thing could happen.

Later that day the bodies of the Sinclair men were recovered but of Hughie Brown's body there was no sign. The funerals of the Sinclair men took place and weeks went past with men searching the shores looking for Hughie's body.

News of this tragedy reached Unst and Mina Robertson was told. She had never fully recovered from the disappointment that Hughie Brown had caused in her life but she was not bitter. She spent much of her time alone. She was not a hermit but she preferred her own company and she went for long walks in the hills whenever the weather allowed. One morning she decided to walk along the shore because the weather seemed uncertain.

There is a beautiful beach near her home, a place where her and her fiancé walked in the days when she was 'on the heads of marriage'. There had been quite a period of gales and the beach was piled high with seaweed.

She noticed one pile higher than the rest and in it was an old boot. Out of curiosity she pulled the seaweed away only to look straight into the dead, distorted and partly decomposed face of Hughie Brown.

21

The Half Gruney Lasses

Joan and Annie Williamson were sisters who worked as servants to the laird who lived in the big house on Uyea Isle. Uyea Isle lies off the south coast of Unst in Shetland and it is a fertile island, a really good place to rear cattle and sheep.

The laird was a powerful man and,by local standards, rich. He owned a large amount of land. Some of this he farmed and some was occupied by tenants who paid rent for their holdings. He also owned fishing boats and had fishermen going far out to sea fishing for cod, ling and tusk.

The laird also owned the island of Half Gruney, which lies to the east of Uyea Isle and to the southeast of Unst itself. Half Gruney is a brilliant, emerald colour especially in the summer. The grass is rich and nutritious. It has long been valued as a place to fatten cattle before slaughter; Half Gruney is a local byword for anyone who is looking their very best.

In the summer of 1745 the aird departed with the usual use of the island. Instead of having animals there to fatten he put in two milking cows.

It was part of the daily duties of the Williamson sisters that they had to go and milk the cows every day. They were skilled in boat handling, and to row across from Uyea Isle normally took no more than ten or fifteen minutes.

The morning of 4 August started off in the way that most other days started for the sisters. They were up early working around the farm and looking after other animals. After a mid-morning break for blaand (whey) and an oatmeal brünnie they set off for Half Gruney.

The cows were well used to Joan and Annie and they had no trouble in catching them and one kept the cow still while the other did the milking. With such good grazing the cows had a lot of milk to give, the fill of three wooden buckets.

The girls were always conscious of any signs of bad weather. The trip between the two islands is not that far but with the wind and tide it can be a rough piece of water. They noticed that the wind was strengthening and from the worst possible direction.

They saw plainly that they would have to row against the wind all the way back and they did not look forward to the journey. They finished the milking as quickly as they could, put the buckets into the boat and lost no time in casting off.

Progress against the strong to gale force wind was slow but the girls were young and powerful rowers and they were entirely confident that they would get back to Uyea Isle safely. Out in the open the wind seemed stronger than ever and it was here that serious misfortune occurred.

Joan's oar snapped just above the blade, leaving her with no more than the thin piece of the oar. In no time at all the boat turned broadside onto the wind and sea.

They had no spare oar, no means of propelling the boat and they knew full well that with the wind and tide as it was they had no chance of drifting back to Half Gruney. They looked at each other helplessly as Unst and the islands faded into the distance.

They were at the mercy of the wind and tide but they knew that they were going in a roughly easterly direction and the next land in that direction was Norway. The day wore on and there was no sighting of any vessel that might rescue them.

They felt so helpless and cursed their stupidity that they did not take a spare oar with them. Towards night the wind dropped and they lay down in the bottom of the boat and tried to rest. The rolling of the boat was now gentle and despite themselves they both fell asleep.

In a northern summer the nights are short and they woke feeling very cold, hungry and in despair. They could see no land and they had no timepiece. Neither did they have any food but they drank some of the milk. They could only sit in the boat and hope against hope for rescue.

The ordeal was to last for eight long days before they saw a smudge on the horizon. The milk was all finished and the last of it was sour and unappetizing. The sun rising and setting was their only way of judging the time or direction.

With nothing to take a bearing on they did not know if they were moving or static in the ocean. It took hours before they could be sure what the mark on the horizon was, but with painful slowness land came into sight; yet they had no way of knowing where they were.

They were seen by people on the shore and when they came within shouting distance they called for help. Although they did not fully understand what was said to them they knew that they were in Norway and that they were not welcome.

The Norwegians thought that they were witches who had had to flee for their lives and they wanted nothing to do with witches on their island. Understanding this, Annie stood up in the boat and made the sign of the cross to indicate that they were Christians.

They landed and a Norwegian woman took them to her house and gave them food and water. Some folk in Shetland could still speak the old language, Norn, and the Williamsons had enough Norn that they could converse, albeit with difficulty.

They told their story and they were made welcome. Of course the Williamson lasses had no money or possessions but the Norwegian woman said that she had recently been widowed and if they were willing to help her with her farm she would keep them as long as they wanted to stay.

As it turned out they never returned to Shetland, the folk there gave them up for lost. They learned to speak the Norwegian language and they both married Norwegian men and had families. In the twenty-first century there are many folk from many different places who claim to be descended from the Half Gruney lasses.

22

Gibby Law

Gibby Law was a young man who lived of the west side of the Shetland Mainland. He was a landowner, not a very rich or powerful one, but a laird nonetheless, with land and tenants to his name.

He was a big, strong, handsome man and the most eligible bachelor in the parish, but he had been born with one defect. One of his eyes was bright blue and farsighted but the other eye was blind.

It had a thick, grey, opaque film covering it and there was no chance of any help for it. Being born like this he found it no great inconvenience, it was the way he was. One year, at the New Year soiree, he announced his engagement to the girl that he had been courting for some time.

It came as no surprised to the community. She was from another village on the other side of the hills, and she and Gibby Law had been seen together at a number of gatherings. Everyone wished them well and said they made a handsome couple.

But Gibby Law had a rival. His name was Simon Arthurson and when he got news of the betrothal he was heard to say through gritted teeth, 'She'll never marry him.'

In the weeks that followed, Gibby was in the habit of walking across the hills to see his fiancée on a regular basis. One night Simon Arthurson got wind of such a visit and he lay in ambush.

There was no road and the place he chose was at the bottom of a dale with steep sides and no more than a narrow sheep's path leading down and up the other side. A burn ran through the dale and Arthurson hid behind a large rock near it.

When he broke cover and confronted Gibby Law the surprise was total. There was little said by either of the men, but a fierce, no holds barred fight at close quarters broke out. In grappling with each other they lost their footing and both rolled into the burn.

Gibby Law was the bigger and stronger man and he was on top, holding down Arthurson. Simon Arthurson thought that Gibby Law was going to hold his head under the water and drown him. He panicked and drew the knife that he was wearing in his belt.

He stabbed upwards and Gibby Law slumped on top and the burn turned red with his blood. Arthurson crawled out and saw, to his horror, that Gibby Law was dead, the knife had gone into his heart.

He had never intended to commit murder but this was what he had done and given that himself and Gibby Law were sworn enemies he did not fancy his chances if he confessed to the crime.

He dragged the corpse out of the water and with a super human effort he managed to carry it up the path to the moorland above. As fast as he could run he went home to his own croft and picked up a spade.

Going back to the dead man he dug a grave and buried Gibby Law in the hope that the body would never be found. It was more than a week before any alarm was raised.

Gibby Law's fiancée did not know that he had set out to see her and his folk did not know that he had failed to reach his destination. A full-scale search was eventually undertaken but without any success.

It was not unknown for someone to fall over a cliff and be swallowed up by the ocean and after weeks of looking, folk began to believe that this might be the case. Life for Gibby Law's fiancée and his parents was never going to be the same again but eventually they learnt to get on with their lives. Gibby Law's dog, however, never gave up the search. He would go out every day, some nights he never came back home. Sometimes only hunger would drive him back. He became as thin as a rake but he persisted; hour after hour and day after day he sought his master.

It was mid-May, the crops were all planted and men were in the hills cutting peats. Two men working together had stopped for a rest and a smoke when Gibby Law's dog came to them barking in a most excited manner.

At first they ignored him but he would not give up and he tugged at the trousers of one of the men. He seemed as if he was trying to tell them something, so the man followed him. When the dog stopped, sat down and barked louder than ever it dawned on the man that the dog had led him to Gibby Law's grave. When the grave was made it was winter and the ground was wet, now in early summer it had dried up and the turf covering the remains had shrunk. The gaps between the turfs had opened and he could see cloth underneath. He called for his friend to come and the two of them took off the soil to reveal the partly decomposed corpse of Gibby Law.

They went back to the village and told the minister. At that time the church looked after all aspects of community life. There was no police presence and the church concerned themselves with civil matters as well as spiritual and moral matters.

It was customary for a dead body to be laid out so that men could pay their last respects. As a mark of respect they touched the forehead of the dead person as they filed past. Of course, Simon Arthurson had to do this too. If he had stayed away he would immediately be suspected. He knew that the minister and the elders were watching very closely, looking for signs that someone might be guilty.

Arthurson was extremely nervous and his hands were shaking, so he kept them in his pockets until the last minute, but despite his efforts to act normally it all went wrong for him. When he attempted to touch Gibby's forehead his hand shook until he poked Gibby Law's eye, the eye that had always been blind.

He broke the opaque film covering the eye and a single tear of blood ran down the dead man's face. At this, Simon Arthurson broke down and confessed that it was he who had killed Gibby Law. He told the authorities the whole story and he was given a trial. The trial had an entirely predictable result. Simon Arthurson was found guilty and he was sentenced to death. After he was hanged his head was cut off.

The head was put into a basket and given into the care of an old woman. She was one who had no means of supporting herself, and was said to be 'on the parish' – that is she was given a small pension to buy essentials with. In return for this she was expected to do jobs around the place. In this case she was instructed to take the basket with Simon Arthurson's head to every house in the parish to show them what happened to wrongdoers. She had a cloth that covered the head and at every house she would take it off with a flourish and say, 'See ye whit I hae!'

23

Sheep Thieves

It was in the year 1469 that Shetland became part of Scotland. It passed from Denmark when the king of Denmark's daughter, Margaret, married King James III of Scotland. It took the best part of one hundred years before Scottish rule effectively kicked in.

When Mary, Queen of Scots returned to Scotland from France to claim the throne she appointed her half-brother, Robert, as governor of Orkney and Shetland. Hand in hand with all this came the Reformation and the iron rule of the Scottish Presbyterian kirk.

The kirk session dealt with all matters of morality and, in the days before a police force, they dealt with many civil matters as well. Shetland was a place where few crimes were committed but there was, from time to time, instances of sheep stealing.

Sheep thieves were nearly always desperate men who had no other means of feeding their starving families; they were seldom men who were out for financial gain. Nonetheless they were punished severely whenever they were caught and this was for a number of reasons: a sheep thief would not steal from anyone who was poor like himself, he would steal from the landlord, the laird, and from anyone who had plentiful sheep. The landowners were also the ruling classes and it was they who were the sheriffs and meted out the punishments.

Sheep thieves seriously offended the kirk. As well as it being a sin to steal – the commandments forbid it – sheep stealing was often done on a Sunday. The Sabbath and Sunday observance was the cornerstone of the kirk's preaching.

Sunday was a popular day to steal sheep because, in those days, nearly everyone went to the kirk, sermons were long and a thief could be confident that he was not going to be seen by anyone. Failure to attend the kirk could be explained away by illness or the illness of a child that had to be looked after. After the act was done a sheep thief had a good chance of getting away with it. During a harsh Shetland winter the loss of an animal could easily be explained away as having failed to survive the winter. However, whenever a sheep thief *was* caught they were shown little mercy. The fact that they had a house full of starving children cut no ice at all.

On the island of Unst there was the case of a man who was convicted of stealing two sheep. His punishment was that he was to be stripped naked and flogged outside every dwelling house in the parish boundaries. That done he was to be taken to the parish boundary, have both his ears cut off to mark him as a thief, and be banished from the island for the rest of his life. To return was to risk hanging.

Another man in North Yell was caught when his wife informed on him. She wanted to be rid of him because she was having an affair with another man. The ranselmen (the forerunners of a police force) investigated the case on a Sunday evening and the thief had slaughtered the sheep in the kitchen of their cottage when they arrived. Always on the alert, the thief heard the horses hooves and as quick as a flash he put the carcase of the sheep into the bed beside his wife who had retired early.

At first the ranselmen found nothing, and for them to violate a lady's bed was unthinkable. But the woman lifted the blankets slightly, just enough for one of the ranselmen to see the wool of the sheep.

The sheep thief was put on trial and it was stated that the crime had been carried out during the time of the kirk service. The sheep that he had stolen and killed belonged to the laird and to add insult to injury he had used the laird's dog to round up the sheep.

He had the bottom part of his ears cut off to mark him as a thief, he was banished from Yell for the rest of his life and he was appointed Demster at the court in Lerwick where, among other duties, he was the hangman.

In the north of the Shetland Mainland there was a famous sheep thief called Johnnie Mann. He lived in the village of Sullom and some say that he was very unscrupulous, he did not care who he stole sheep from so long as they were fat and made good eating.

One winter night he came to grief while out on a sheep-stealing expedition. The evidence was that he had taken a shortcut across a frozen loch, as the surface of the ice had a powdering of snow and footprints could be clearly seen, as well as the paw prints of a dog.

Johnnie Mann's dog was what was known as a gripper. He did not seek to round up sheep as modern dogs do, but would chase a sheep, grip the hind leg in his teeth and tip it over. The dog would hold on tenuously until his master arrived to take hold of the sheep.

On that fatal night, Johnnie Mann had caught two sheep and taken them on his back with a view to carrying them home. However, when he made the return journey across the loch the ice broke and he was found some days later drowned with the sheep still on his back.

His body was laid out inside a nearby mill; it was not taken to his home or to a kirk. It was the custom that when someone died an unusual death, or any corpse that came with the sea, they would be buried close to where they were found.

That very night Dr Driver had been in the north of the island attending a difficult birth. Dr Driver rode a milk white horse and covered a large area in his work as a healer of the sick. In this case the baby was born and the mother and the child were well.

Dr Driver was in good humour, it was great satisfaction to him that he had done a good job, and it was always good to see a new life come into the world. But he was tired, it was midnight and he had had a long day.

His horse was tired too and he stopped at the mill that contained Johnnie Mann's corpse. Another man might have been uncomfortable so close to death but not Dr Driver. He was a man of medicine and science and a corpse held no terrors for him. He was also addicted to snuff and one of the reasons why he had stopped at the mill was that it gave him shelter to open his snuffbox. To open a

snuff box in the wind was to risk having it all blow away. Looking at the door of the mill he addressed Johnnie Mann flippantly.

'Come out here you bugger and take snuff with me,' he ordered.

He was astonished when, a few seconds later, the door of the mill opened and the most terrifying apparition appeared and made straight for the horse; it appeared that it was going to grip the reins. The horse was so terrified that he bolted with the good doctor still on his back. The horse ran, out of control, until he was exhausted. Luckily for him and his rider he stopped on the edge of a very high cliff; another few strides would have taken them both to their deaths.

It took them a long time to make their way home but the slow journey gave Dr Driver the opportunity to calm down and think rationally once more. The need for comfort from his snuffbox was great and he found that the pinch of snuff that he was about to take outside the mill door was still between his forefinger and thumb.

One sheep thief who was a native of the west side of the Shetland Mainland was an outlaw in every sense of the word. He lived in a cave in the middle of an inaccessible cliff and he was never seen in the daytime.

He would climb up to the top of the cliff at night and steal a sheep but he had other needs too and he would steal whatever he could that was of any use to him. When he had caught a sheep he would tie its legs with a long rope and lower it from a spur of rock that overhung the cliff onto a ledge that was outside the entrance of his cave.

Once he abducted a boy from the village, with the aim to make the young lad his apprentice so that when he was old and less fit the boy would carry on his illegal work and allow him to live in the way that he had always done.

The boy had no option but to go along with the thief but he was always on the lookout for a way of escaping. He persuaded the sheep thief that he was committed to a life of crime and he suggested that they raid his own home.

He told the sheep thief that his father had valuables and it was agreed that they would make a raid. When they arrived at the croft the boy shouted for help and the sheep thief was overpowered and brought to justice and the boy was free to live with his parents once more.

Just as people from the North East of England are known as 'Geordies' and Liverpudlians are known as 'Scousers' so people from the island of Yell in Shetland are known locally as 'Sheep thieves'. Another case of sheep stealing is told about a family that lived in Heatherdale.

The old name for Heatherdale is Glippapund, but no matter what it is called it is one of the most beautiful places in Shetland. It is situated at the head of Gloup Voe, the nearest thing to a Norwegian fjord in Shetland. The valley is deep with a burn running through it, surrounded by high hills and glens. It is sheltered and isolated and it is not surprising that some folk saw it as being an attractive place to live. However, it did have two major disadvantages: it was not an ideal place to keep a boat and the land was not fertile. One family who lived there was one of the last two families to speak the old language, Norn.

One day a Ranselman called at Heatherdale to look for any evidence of sheep stealing. He dismounted from his horse and spoke to the woman of the house, who happened to be the mother of the family who still spoke Norn.

She was at home by herself with several children, her husband was away fishing she said. The Ranselman could see nothing suspicious and decided that there was nothing more that he could do. He was about to leave when he noticed a young boy, at a short distance from the door of the house, playing with a sheep's head.

He snatched the sheep's head from the boy and a quick glance at the earmarks told him that the sheep had belonged to the laird. He jumped on his horse but the woman saw him taking the sheep's head and she tried to pull him off his horse.

He managed to push her away but she got hold of the horse tail and clung on for dear life. She screamed at the Ranselman in the Norn language and he knew what she was saying: 'Speak well of Glippapund's men, speak well of Glippapund's men.'

As the horse gained speed and she was being dragged along she had to let go. The Ranselman had obtained all the evidence he needed to make a case of sheep stealing against the family. The following morning a whole posse of Ranselmen descended on the quiet valley only to find it empty.

The family had gone and they had taken all their possessions with them. The Ranselmen thought that perhaps they had flit to Trootis, the place where the other Norn-speaking family lived, but they had gone too. No one knew where they went and neither family was ever seen in Yell again.

There were three brothers who lived deep in the hills near the small lochs known as the Grud Waters, who were also suspected of sheep stealing. None of those men were ever married and they lived in a miserable hovel made from earth.

The house, such as it was, had no chimney, just a hole in the middle of the thatch to let the smoke escape. It was easy for the Ranselmen to keep watch on them: one of their number would quietly climb on to the roof and look down through the smoke hole.

One night what the Ranselman saw was that one of the brothers had been fishing. They were cooking sillocks, small coal fish that could be caught off the rocks. They also had a small pan of fish livers, the soft roe, they had been melted down to fish oil.

The fish was served up in a big wooden bowl and the liver oil poured over them. The brothers had no plates and no cutlery: they ate with their fingers. But before they started the oldest brother said grace, and he asked a blessing. He said, 'May God grant that the thief never knows how honest men live.'

The Ranselmen never spied on them again.

24

The First Midges

Once upon a time there was a very wicked giant who killed and ate children. He lived on a skerry out in the sea but when the tide was out a causeway was exposed and the giant could walk from his home on the rock on to the main island. Everyone knew when he arrived, as he would shout in a very loud voice, 'I'm coming to eat you!'

He would then grab a child, if he could, and go back to his skerry and the poor child was never seen again. All the parents were determined to protect their precious children; they hated the giant and they made plans to put a stop to his raids.

There was one fourteen-year-old boy who was a very fast runner and they decided that they needed him to help with their plans.

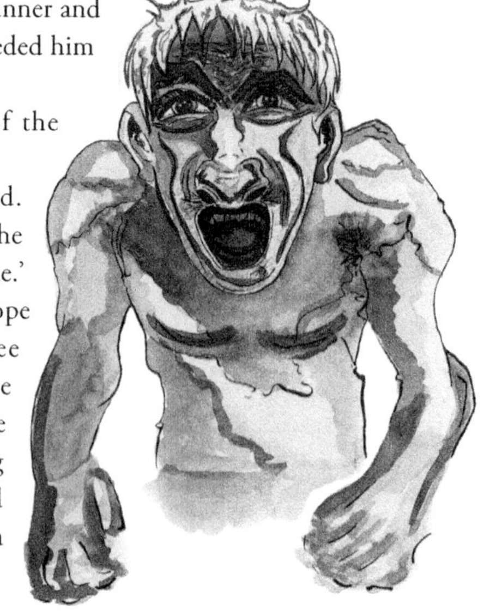

'Are you frightened of the giant?' they asked him.

'Not me,' he answered. 'I can run far faster than he can – he will never catch me.'

The men stretched a rope across the beach. Three strong men hid in the clump of rocks below the high water mark holding one end of the rope and another three men hid in a geo holding the other end.

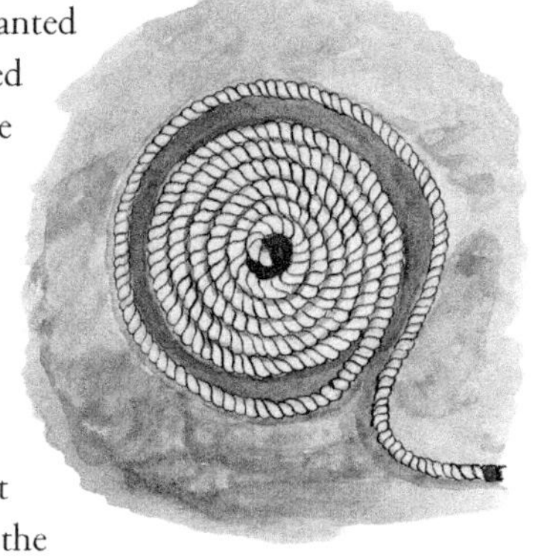

The boy knew exactly what they wanted him to do and when the giant shouted that he was coming to eat him the boy shouted back, 'You are too old, too ugly, too stupid, too slow and you will never catch me.'

He had two stones in his hands, both about the size of an egg. He threw the first one and hit the giant a painful blow in the head. But that was nothing to the second one; it hit the giant, with a crack, on the nose.

The giant was furious and began to chase the boy along the beach. He crossed the rope and when the giant got near they pulled the rope tight and the giant tripped over it, fell flat on his face and ploughed up the beach with his sore nose.

This was the moment that they all had waited for. Men came from all direction armed with knives, hay forks, scythe blades and clubs and they all attacked the giant. A big man with a scythe blade cut off his head and they were sure that they had finished off the giant.

They were all so happy because this meant that the giant would never again eat a child. They all danced around, chanting,

'We've killed the giant, we've killed the giant!'

However, as the huge head rolled down the beach the voice came again, 'I'm coming to eat you!'

They could not believe it but it was unmistakeable. So they set to work again and they cut the giant into far smaller pieces, and again they sang, 'We've killed the giant. We've killed the giant!'

But the loud voice came again, 'I'm coming to eat you!'

Everyone was baffled as they knew that they had done much damage to the giant but they did not trust him so they set about cutting him into smaller and smaller pieces. By the time that they had done that they were all exhausted but they raised a cheer and shouted as one, 'We've killed the giant! We've killed the giant!'

But again the voice came back, 'I'm coming to eat you!'

No one could understand it but they were determined to put an end to the giant once and for all. They began to gather all the driftwood from the beach and some went to get baskets of peats and they used all this to make a big fire.

Bit by bit the giant was burned: fingers, hands, toes, legs, ears, nose. Two men rolled the head into the fire along with yards and yards of guts. The giant was so big that it took all night to burn all of him.

Several times they had to gather more driftwood and peat, but at last he was all gone. When dawn broke there was nothing left, just the dying embers of the fire and a heap of grey ashes.

Exhausted as they were they found the energy to have one last cheer. They all danced around the remains of the fire chanting, 'We've killed the giant! We've killed the giant!'

At that moment there came a strong gust of wind which blew the ashes from the fire up in the air and the giant's voice came again, 'I'm coming to eat you!'

Each and every fleck of ash turned into a midge and, of course, they have been eating us ever since.

25

Da Hallamas Mareel

At the Burgi Geo in northwest Yell there lies the remains of an Iron Age fort. It is on a headland joined to the rest of the island by a narrow neck of land. There are rows of standing stones that lead, on one side, into the fort, but on the other side the standing stones lead the unwary over the high cliff and to their doom.

Long after the original inhabitants left, the fort was taken over by a ruthless and cruel band of Vikings who preyed on the honest and hardworking udallers: West-A-Firth, in those days, was a wild and lawless place.

It was late autumn and the children of West-A-Firth were preparing for Hallamas. Wearing the traditional straw hats, they had been to every house in the area collecting money the taditional party that took place every year. All the houses that is, save one. It was a miserable hovel deep in the hills, where the Spaeman, the hermit Isaac Omand, lived. He welcomed no one and no one knew how he made a living. If he was ever heard speaking it was always in riddles that no one could understand.

All the money collected for Hallamas was given to Mary. She was a spinster who lived alone but she loved children and she was always to the fore at Hallamas time. Along with Martha Rassusson and Jenny Ninian she went to the shop at Glippapund to buy the food for the party.

For the rest of the week they baked fatty bannocks, currney buns, oven sliddericks and dumplings. They made tattie soup they kirned for fresh butter, kirn milk and blaand. A lamb had been butchered and meat and mealy puddings were cooked.

When Mary returned home after visiting a neighbour she was distraught to find that the robbers from the Burgi Geo had raided the house and taken everything. On being told, the Oldest Udaller called a meeting and the folk came from Setter, the Neap, Graven and Vigon to discuss what they could do.

There was no question of confronting the Vikings; they were far too powerful and to try and fight them meant the certain loss of life. Sadly there were no suggestions and most were resigned to their fate.

'Der only da wan thing we kan dü,' declared the Oldest Udaller, 'we maun geng an ax the Spaeman.'

'Der nae öse o dat,' said Sigurd Ollason, 'he'll never spik tae wis an even if he dus we'll nivver keen whit he means.'

In the absence of any other ideas, Sigurd and Tirval Ertirson were sent to consult the Spaeman. When they arrived at his house they got the impression that Isaac Omand was expecting them.

He was outside, a tiny man dressed in rags; he had a long grey beard and he had not washed for a very long time. He never gave them a chance to speak but said in a shrill wavering voice:

Da Burgi Geo men ir fat an greedy
While wis puir fok ir tin an needy
Bit ta mak things rite an weel
Ye maun öse da Hallamas mareel.

So saying, he went inside and shut the door leaving Sigurd and Tirval speechless. Feeling that their journey had been wasted, they made their way back to the house of the Oldest Udaller. They told him the Spaeman's rhyme and waited for his response, which took some time in coming.

'Da only plis it we kan get mareel fae is da sea so sum o you il haeta geng ta da kraigs.'

They saw it as futile but they did as they were told. They took their homemade rods and began fishing from the rocks. When the light began to fade they were astonished at the mareel in the water. They had never seen anything like it: the sea, the fish and the fishing line flashed with ribbons of fire.

On the way home Sigurd suddenly had an idea of how they could use the mareel. He was confident that the robbers would come to steal the fish so he got Tirval and others to skin the piltocks and sillocks. From the womenfolk he got old blankets and pieces of linen and they began to sew the fish skins onto the cloth.

Six men donned the mareel-covered cloth and they set off westwards towards the Burgi Geo but hid below the banks of the burn to keep watch for the robbers. The mareel flashed like green fire in the moonlight.

They did not have to wait long and all the men kept low until Sigurd gave the shout and they all leaped up shouting, jumping and waving their arms. The effect on the robbers was amazing, they were terrified and turned tail and ran back towards the Burgi Geo as fast as they could go.

The West-A-Firth men followed, screaming and shouting. The robbers, in their panic, followed the wrong set of standing stones and every last one of them disappeared over the cliff to their death.

In the days that followed, the West-A-Firth men ventured into the fort and found it empty of people, but they were able to recover many of the things that the robbers had stolen from them over the years. And so the community enjoyed the best ever Hallamas and they were able to live in peace and with plenty ever after.

26

URSULA

In the year 1890, James Williamson was one of the most predominant and respected citizens of Laxwick. He was an Elder of the kirk and a member of the kirk session. The kirk session saw it as their duty to seek out and eliminate all sinful practices in the parish.

James Williamson was a very stern man and he was foremost among those who were upholders of Christian and moral values. No one was allowed to do any work on the Sabbath unless it was unavoidable, like feeding livestock. If anything had to be carried on a Sunday, it had to be in the arms, never on the back.

Attendance at Sunday worship was obligatory, regardless of the weather, and on Sundays music other than the Psalms was forbidden, and no reading material could be looked at except the Bible or the *Christian Herald*. Breaking the Sabbath was a serious offence, and any person guilty of such had to repent their sins and mend their ways.

Youngsters were given severe instruction in regard to behaviour, and in addition to the kirk services they were sent to Sunday school. The popular belief was, very definitely, that any sparing of the rod certainly spoilt the child.

It was young women who could commit the worst and most damning of all sins, namely antinuptial fornication (as any sexual activity out of wedlock was so described). Any girl who was unmarried but became pregnant was guilty of this crime.

Any such girl would have to appear, along with other sinners, before the kirk session and be forced to tell who the father of her unborn child was and where the fornication took place. The man

involved would be compelled to marry the girl. That would ease the situation.

However, if the man absconded, the girl would have to shoulder all the blame and her name would appear on the kirk door. She would be shamed and her child would be known as a bastard. It was a stigma; she would live in the shadow of her grave sin for a great many years to come.

Ministers, too, came under considerable pressure from men like James Williamson. The upstander, as the minister was sometimes known, and his wife were expected to lead Spartan, blameless lives. Sunday services lasted anything up to three hours and sermons were stern and vehement in content.

Any minister who had notes in the pulpit or read his sermons was considered grossly incompetent. One nervous young preacher who was seen to be reading from notes overheard one member of the congregation say to another, 'It was read, it wasn't well read and it wasn't worth reading!'

Every Sabbath there were two services in the kirk as well as the Sunday school for the children. On weekdays the minister had to visit his parishioners, especially the old and infirm folk who were unable to attend church. Sometimes the minister and his wife were required to give medical and even veterinary advice. Ministers enjoyed a higher place in the community, in terms of esteem, than anyone except, perhaps, the laird.

The parish minister of Laxwick was the Revd R. Norman Farquhar and he was exactly the kind of minister that James Williamson approved of. An energetic man in his forties, he was entirely fundamentalist in his views and relentless in his determined purge against the Devil, sin and all things evil.

Mrs Farquhar was a model of moral values, she knew something of medicine and she would distribute tonics and cough cures to ailing people in the parish. The Revd Farquhar's sermons were so dire in their warnings that listeners gasped and quaked in the pews and no one dared fall asleep.

It was in this kind of a society that young Ursula Williamson grew up. She was eighteen and had blossomed into a lovely young woman. She was small and slim with red hair and green eyes; she had a most attractive and ready smile that made her beautiful.

She worked with her father on the croft. She raised peats, pulled harrows, hoed fields of potatoes and turnips and worked among the sheep and cattle. Her father, in keeping with his character, was a hard taskmaster, but Ursula never complained, she was always willing and cheerful.

James Williamson erected a puritanical wall around his daughter that was a serious deterrent to even the boldest suitor. Ursula had many admirers but getting the approval of James Williamson was an impossible dream; he was just too formidable, too forbidding.

It was with disbelief that Mrs Joan Williamson noticed a change come over Ursula. She tried to ignore what she saw but eventually she came to the inescapable conclusion that her daughter was pregnant. One day, when John was away on some business or other, she talked to Ursula.

Ursula's response was to burst into tears, confirming Mrs Williamson's worst fears. She asked Ursula no questions; she knew that plenty of questions would come from her husband and the kirk session.

When James Williamson was told his reaction was entirely predictable. He was furious. He demanded to know who the man was but Ursula refused to tell him and so the matter was reported to the kirk session. The session clerk convened a meeting of the session and Ursula was summonsed to attend. James would not even afford his daughter the comfort of allowing her to walk with him to the kirk.

They made their separate ways to the kirk, where the meeting was held in the vestry. It was a cold, bleak room. Portraits of previous incumbents adorned the walls: solemn, unsmiling men with formal dress and collars. Ursula was not offered a seat and she had to stand in front of them all.

For hours on end she was interrogated but she steadfastly refused to say who the father of her unborn child was. At a late hour, Mr Farquhar suggested that Ursula be sent home for the night to pray and reflect. She was to appear again in two days' time. Ursula was no more forthcoming on that occasion. It was only on the third night of questioning that Ursula finally broke down.

In a small tearful voice that was barely audible she named the Revd R. Norman Farquhar. If her plight was bad before, it was now ten times worse. They all turned on her like a pack of wolves. Farquhar himself was outraged.

'How dare you,' he roared in a voice full of menace. 'How dare you accuse me, a happily married man and a man of God, of adultery. I would not soil myself on you. You are a liar and a harlot. You are a wicked lass that has been made profoundly ugly by your terrible sin. Tonight and in the nights to come I will pray for you but you should spend the rest of your life on your knees begging for forgiveness and salvation.'

Ignoring Ursula's sobbing and wailing, the members of the session, one by one, pitilessly condemned her; not one showed even the tiniest hint of compassion for her great distress, pain and discomfort. Her father was the last to speak.

'All my life,' he emotionally declared, 'I have tried to follow in the footsteps of God.'

Looking up to Heaven he continued, 'I implore you, tell me what I have done that I deserve to father such a creature.'

Looking directly at Ursula for the first time, he told her coldly, 'I no longer consider you to be my daughter; you have ruined and defiled everything that I stand for and no longer are you welcome under my roof.'

Mrs Williamson was heartbroken, but there was nothing she could do but help Ursula to pack up her few possessions in readiness to leave home. Mrs Williamson gave Ursula everything that she could and she gave her all the money that she had. The farewell was the saddest day in the lives of both mother and daughter.

Before she left, Ursula spoke to her father one last time. She was calm and controlled.

'Father,' she said, 'what I told the kirk session was true, Farquhar is a liar and a hypocrite.' James Williamson had his mouth open to interrupt.

'No father,' said Ursula, 'you have never, in my life, listened to anything that I had to say but you will, whether you like it or not, hear this. Farquhar is the man who put me in the family way. It happened one Sunday when I had been helping with the Sunday school.

'When all the children had gone we were left alone. I gave him no encouragement, I tried to fight him off but he was too strong for me. This that has happened is not my fault; it is his and his alone. No other man ever laid a finger on me.

'I don't suppose that you will believe me even now but I will tell you one last thing. I want everyone to hear this; before I die there will be a sign that will tell all of Laxwick that I have told the truth. I will be vindicated.'

Ursula Williamson left Laxwick and made her way, by stages, to Leith, where she found refuge with a widowed aunt. Ursula kept in touch with friends back home but she never returned and she never saw Laxwick, or her father, again.

More than sixty years later a student minister arrived in Laxwick. He was Andrew Danielson and he about to embark on his final year at college. He had been sent to Laxwick for two reasons, firstly to gain pastoral experience and secondly to fill a gap while the parish minister was on holiday.

Andrew had the manse to himself but he looked forward to the challenge of conducting a service all by himself. On his first Sunday morning he was nervous and restless and he added more and more finishing touches to his sermon. About an hour before the service was due to start he had occasion to go into the vestry of the kirk.

His eye was immediately drawn to the broken glass on the floor. One of the portraits, of a previous parish minister, had fallen off the wall. The frame was more diamond shaped than oblong and the thin glass had shattered. Andrew took a brush and a fire shovel and swept up the debris.

He took it outside and poured the broken glass into a hole in the dry stone dyke. Old Jacob, an Elder who lived nearby, came to see what Andrew was doing. The standards of Sunday observance had relaxed somewhat but he did not like to see the young preacher doing work on the Sabbath.

Andrew told him about the picture falling off the wall and how he was merely trying to clear up the mess.

'It's Farquhar's likeness isn't it?' asked Jacob.

'I haven't a clue,' replied Andrew. 'Their whiskery old faces all look the same to me.'

The two of them went back into the vestry and, right enough, lying half in and half out of the frame was the Revd R. Norman Farquhar's portrait.

'How on earth did you know that it was Farquhar who fell down?' asked Andrew.

Jacob paused a moment and stroked his white beard.

'It was sure to be Farquhar,' he said. 'Ursula Williamson died last night.'

27

THE MOUSE AND THE WREN

Once upon a time there was a mouse and a wren that shared the same home. Home to them was a dry stone dyke that surrounded a farmyard. In normal times they were friends and lived happily together but on one hard winter's day they had a serious quarrel.

The ground was frozen and food was very scarce. The few seeds that had been blown into the dyke during the autumn had all been eaten and they were both very hungry. The wren found a seed or two and gobbled them up without offering any to the mouse.

The mouse was very angry and told the wren that she was selfish.

'You have wings,' he said. 'Why don't you fly away and find food, I can't fly and you never spare a thought for me who is stranded on the ground.'

The wren did not like being labelled as selfish and she gave the mouse a sharp peck, near his eye, with her beak.

'Now you are trying to blind me,' the mouse squeaked loudly, and he bit the wren in the wing and that was very painful. Soon the two of them were engaged in a pitched battle with hair and feathers flying.

The mouse, with his sharp teeth, was getting the better of things and a passing sparrow, attracted by the noise, saw what was going on and decided that the wren needed help. The two birds were getting the better of the mouse until a rat came to help the mouse.

A starling joined in as well as a rabbit, a blackbird, stoat, a dove, a hedgehog, wakened from his sleep, a gull, a cat, a skua, a dog, and an eagle. Soon every animal and bird was fighting in the biggest battle that you can ever imagine.

There were two creatures that refused to fight and they were the fox and the owl. The fox would not join in because he wanted to know who was going to win; he wanted to be on the winning side. The wise old owl, on the other hand, would not join in because he knew that the fighting was stupid, no one would gain anything from it.

'When you have all calmed down and come to your senses I will be the judge. I will tell you who has won and who has lost,' he said.

The fox jumped up on the dyke to get a good view.

'I will tell you all who is winning,' he said. 'If my tail is up in the air and waving that will tell you that the animals are winning but if my tail is down between my legs that will show that the birds are having the better of things.'

There was no doubt that the animals were winning. The birds were having a tough time, definitely losing and the fox's tail was waving in the air. At this time a swarm of bees arrived on the scene. They saw that the birds were going to lose the fight and because they too had wings they were on the side of the birds.

'What can we do to help the birds?' asked one bee. 'We are only small insects.' The leader of the bees had a plan. He told them all to gather around and he told them what he had in mind. Thirty of the biggest and strongest bees flew off towards the fox. His tail was still waving high in triumph until all at once the bees stung him in the bum.

The fox gave a howl of agony and tucked his tail between his legs to try and soothe the pain. When the birds saw that the fox's tail was down they thought that they must be winning. When the animals saw that the fox's tail was down they thought that they must be losing.

And so it was, everyone was exhausted and the fighting stopped. It was time for the owl's verdict.

'Here is my judgement,' said the owl in his most dulcet voice. 'The birds have won the fight and they therefore have the right to fly through the air or sit on the ground. The animals lost the fight so they are condemned to stay on the ground for all time to come.'

And so it has been ever since.

28

Ruud

Rögnvald and his stepfather, Thorolf, were bitter enemies and they never missed an opportunity to do each other a bad turn. Their hatred of each other came to a head when Rögnvald burned Thorolf's house down and everyone in it perished.

His own son, Gunnar, was being fostered in the house but Rögnvald took him to safety before he started the fire. Father and son watched the house burning and Gunnar said to his father, 'Far rather would I burn in that house with my foster father than be here with you. When you have dealt so ill with him I know that you will not deal well with me.'

Rögnvald did not want anyone to know that he was the one who started the fire and he did not trust his son, who was still a child, not to tell others. He took the boy and tied him to the mast of a boat and set it adrift to be taken away by the wind and the tide.

Eventually the boat ran aground on another island far to the north and he was found by a rich and powerful man who ruled there. The man followed the old gods and made the sacrifices to them in the way that had been done for many generations.

This ruler questioned the boy about who he was and why he had been so cruelly treated but the boy would tell him nothing.

The man admired the boy's courage and because he was wearing a red coat he called him Ruud. The man adopted Ruud as his son, and he grew up to be a strong, handsome man. His adoptive father loved him so much that he left all his land and possessions to Ruud when he died. This included a great temple dedicated to the god Thor. Ruud kept up all the sacrifices and every day he spoke to the idol that was made in Thor's image. So dedicated was Ruud to the idol that it began to speak back to him and follow him around the island.

One morning Thor refused to speak to Ruud and he could not understand why. Ruud tried everything he knew to get speech out of Thor and at last he got a response when Thor made a big sigh. 'I am not silent without good cause,' he said. 'I am greatly distressed by the men who are on their way to this island.'

'Who are they?' asked Ruud.

'It is the king and his men. They are coming to Christianise the whole of this area.'

Ruud told him that they would fight to keep them away but Thor said it was no use, they were stronger than he was.

'Come with me to the shore and blow mightily through the bristles of your beard and you will raise such a storm that the king will never get here.'

Thor did not like the idea very much but he agreed to give it a try. They could see the king's longship full of armed warriors. Thor blew the first of three mighty blows and such was the fury of the storm he created that the king had to turn back.

It was the same each day for three days but it made the king ever more determined to reach the island to do his holy work. On the fourth morning, when Ruud went to the temple, he found Thor in a depressed state.

'The king has landed on the island,' he told Ruud.

'Then we will stand against him with all our might,' declared Ruud.

Thor told him that it was no good, the king was stronger than they were. The king summonsed Ruud to come and meet him, but Ruud refused.

'I will not go to meet him for I like not his coming and still less does my mighty god Thor like it.'

The king came to Ruud and called for everyone on the island so that he could preach the Christian faith to them. Still Ruud would not give up the god who had helped him in all his troubles. The king threatened his life if he refused to obey. Ruud suggested that have a trial of their gods.

'I shall make a great fire and you and Thor shall stand on either side of it holding the ends of a chain. The one who pulls the other through the fire shall be the victor and I expect that Thor will be stronger than you.'

The king declared that he had never heard the like before. He said that no man had ever before dared to set up Devils for him to contend with while he preached the Holy Faith. However, he accepted the challenge on condition that no one would help either side.

The fire was prepared and lit and the king and Thor took their places and the struggle began. For a time it looked an even match but Thor slipped and he fell into the fire. The fire consumed him and his body was turned to ashes.

Ruud had to admit that Thor had been defeated and he lost all faith in him. It was soon afterwards that Ruud too became a Christian.

29

The Sad End of Grotti Finnie

The crew of a small sailing ship were in need of fresh water so they anchored in a sheltered bay and two men and a boy rowed ashore with empty kegs. They did not like the first water that they found; it was slightly blackish and did not have a nice taste. They walked further inland where they found a spring where the water was pure, clear and sweet.

They drank their fill and filled the kegs. The two men wanted to rest before they set off back to the ship but the boy was full of energy and he wanted to explore this strange place. He heard a great noise and found that the noise came from a monster that was sleeping beside the loch.

The boy had never seen any living thing so big and he was so curious that he went to take a closer look. It was very ugly and, even if the boy did not know it, it was a troll called Grotti Finnie. Trolls like Grotti Finnie should never be confused with the Shetland trows – they are small, full of mischief and they love music, play fiddles, and dance and sing.

The boy was bold enough to go so close that he could touch the scaly hand of Grotti Finnie but the monster continued to snore and sleep. If he had been a good boy he would have walked away and left Grotti Finnie in peace, but the boy was not all that good. He happened to have a needle with him, which he took and stabbed into Grotti Finnie's belly. The monster wakened with a cry of pain and a jump. He sat up and then said, 'Fee fy foe fum, I smell the blood of an earthly man. Be living or be he dead I'll have his head with my supper bread.'

Attracted by the noise the men arrived on the scene and when they heard what Grotti Finnie said they all ran as fast as they could back to the beach where they had left their boat. Grotti Finnie had been sleeping for a long time, he was stiff and sore, he could not run very fast so the men, and the boy, were well ahead of him. But even if he was slow, the monster had strong legs and he could jump.

He jumped across a valley and had nearly caught them by the time they got the boat launched. Grotti Finnie was determined not to be beat and he reached out his long arm to pull the boat ashore again.

The men saw his scaly hand with the curled fingernails coming over the gunwale of the boat and they feared the worst. The boy snatched up an axe and with a vicious swipe cut Grotti Finnie's hand clean off, and it fell into the sea with a splash.

Grotti Finnie howled and screeched with pain and anger but he would not give up. He ran along the shore to a place where he was nearer to the boat and reached out with his other hand, which was even more ugly than the one that had been chopped off. When this hand reached the boat the boy said, 'Ho ho he only had the two hands to begin with so if I chop this one off too he will not have any left.'

And so he did and there was a huge commotion as Grotti yelled and danced with pain. He wept and howled until his cries could be heard all over the island and it attracted the attention of three other trolls.

They were Tushie, Tangie and Lucky Minnie, a revolting looking threesome who came galloping along to find out what all the noise was about. They gathered around Grotti Finnie and demanded to know what all the lamenting was about.

He told them how he had chased those earthly men across the island and how this cruel, nasty little boy had cut off both his hands. The other trolls had no sympathy with Grotti Finnie.

'Serves you right,' growled Tushie.

'Why did you not tell us?' snarled Tangie.

'Greedy glutton brute,' screamed Lucky Minnie. 'You would have eaten them all yourself and would have given us nothing.'

They began to beat Grotti Finnie. They beat him and beat him until they beat him to pieces. Tushie took one of his legs for a walking stick, Tangie took his arms for flails and Lucky Minnie took his head to make into a teapot. And that was the end of Grotti Finnie.

30

THE CATS AND THE CHRISTENING

Once upon a time there were two cats that lived together and they were great friends. They did everything together and every night they went out hunting and they shared anything they found or caught.

One night they had little success but when it was nearly dawn they managed to steal a big jar of butter. They had no time to eat any of it but they hid it away in a safe place saying that they would go back and retrieve it another night.

The next night one of the cats said that she had been invited to a christening so she went out by herself. She was away a long time and when she returned her friend asked what had happened at the christening and what was the name of the kitten.

She told, in great detail, all that had happened and said that the kitten's name was Well Concealed. The next night the same cat said that she was invited to another christening and she went out by herself again.

When she came back she had another long story to tell and she said the kitten's name was Top Off. The same thing happened again and the cat said that she was going to yet another christening and this time she said that the kitten's name was Half Done.

The cat left at home every night began to be suspicious so the next time that her friend said that she was going to a christening she followed her to see if she was telling the truth. There was no christening, the cat went to the butter that they had hidden together, took off the top and began to eat.

The other cat was furious to find that her friend was cheating her; they had a terrible row and a terrible fight and they were never friends again.

31

Einar the Fowler

Einar was a young man with a grievance. Like many of his friends he was poor, he could hardly make enough to keep food on the table for him and his wife. He was a tenant of a croft, a smallholding and the land he tried to cultivate was poor in quality.

He eked out a living by catching birds in the cliffs when the season was right. But even this was far from easy and it was extremely dangerous. Einar's resentment was against the four big farmers and landowners who kept all the best land and the most productive cliffs for themselves.

True there were cliff areas that belonged to the community, but those did not have as many birds and there were many crofters who went fowling in them. To be caught in the cliffs that the big farmers claimed as belonging to them could risk the most severe punishment. They seemed to control the law as well as everything else.

By common consent, Einar was the best cragsman in the village; he was also the boldest and most daring. Einar had the ability to go to the areas of the cliffs that others found too difficult and too dangerous.

He did not want to appear greedy and take more than his fair share from the cliffs open to everyone and it was widely known that he 'stole' from the cliffs of the farmers. Einar would never concede that it was stealing; in his mind he had as much right to be there as anyone else.

Einar was looking for an opportunity to go to a forbidden cliff where the birds were plentiful. The chance came one fine morning when most of his neighbours went off to the fishing in their boats.

The farmers often worked together and Einar knew that they were going to the moors to work at their peats.

When he thought that the coast was clear he got his net that was fixed on a long pole, his basket and his rope and set off for his chosen cliff. It was the steepest and highest of all the cliffs in the area but Einar knew that it would prove to be productive.

He drove a stout stake deep into the hard earth on the cliff top. He tied his rope to this stake and holding on to it he lowered himself over the edge. The cliff face was sheer with not so much as a claw hold for a bird, and hardly a ledge that a mouse could run along. But Einar knew exactly what he was doing and his feet found the wide ledge that he was to use as his platform. He steadied himself, released his grip on the rope and set about capturing the birds.

Meanwhile the farmers were discussing Einar. They knew that he went to the cliff that they regarded as their own private property and they were determined to catch him and bring him to justice. They would teach him a lesson that would keep him in line in the future.

It came to their attention that all the tenants had gone to the fishing and that Einar had stayed ashore. That could only mean one thing: that he was going to the forbidden cliff. It took them little time to find his rope tied to the stake.

It was slack and this told them that Einar was not holding it so they hauled the rope up to the cliff top. The oldest of the farmers was Einar's bitterest enemy and he said, 'Without a rope there is no way up from where he is, it is impossible for anyone to climb this cliff. We shall leave him where he is all night and we will haul him up in the morning.'

The first hint of trouble for Einar came when a small stone rattled down the cliff face. He knew that someone had to be at the top and he watched with horror as the end of his rope went up the cliff face and out of sight over the top. He knew it had to be the farmers and he knew that he could expect little mercy from them. They might abandon him entirely or they could put the rope back down and cut it while he was using it to climb up the cliff.

He knew that his only hope was to climb the cliff, impossible as that feat might seem. He studied the cliff face and tried to plan a route to the top. He abandoned his catch of birds, he left his pole and net and he took off most of his clothes.

With his bare hands and feet, and dressed in nothing but his shirt, he began to climb. If he had been asked a thousand times he could never tell how he managed it but somehow he reached the top.

He was bruised, bleeding and utterly exhausted and for a time he lay prone, too tired to move. But that would not do either because the farmers were likely to be on the go and likely to visit his house.

He got to his feet. By this time it was dark and he made what speed he could on his way home. He was lucky insofar as he met no one on the way and he got indoors without being seen.

His wife was shocked at the state he was in and that he had no clothes but his shirt. He quickly told her what had happened and said that if the farmers came asking anything about him she was to say that he was in bed sleeping.

The farmers had finished their evening meal and decided to find out what Einar's wife had to say for herself.

When they got to Einar's cottage they went straight in and found his wife tending the fire. With a smile she asked them why they were visiting. The oldest farmer was a spokesman for all of them.

'We have business with Einar.'

'Einar has gone to bed.'

They all grinned in triumph, sure that she was telling a lie. They said that they did not care, they wanted to speak to him anyway. The lady of the house said no more but led them to the bedroom. The farmers exchanged glances, determined that they were not going to be fooled.

Einar had been listening to every word and found it hard not to laugh out loud. He pretended to be asleep and snored loudly while the farmers stood speechless, dumfounded.

'Wake up Einar,' said his wife shaking him. 'The farmers are here to see you.'

Now the farmers had to think of something, some reason for coming to the house. It was the oldest farmer who spoke once again.

'Einar we are here to ask you if you will work for us. We want you to be our fowler, you can go in cliffs where no other man can go and no man can do the job better.'

Einar agreed but he demanded concessions for himself and all the other tenants.

And so it was that the quality of life for the poor crofters improved. When the word spread of Einar's feat of climbing the cliff and the deal he made with the farmers, he won the gratitude and respect of the entire community.

32

ERIK AND THE SHARK

Erik was over sixty years of age but he was fit, muscular and nimble on his feet. His beard and hair were as black as the raven's wing and he could have passed for a man of forty. His face had deep lines no doubt caused by the many lashings of salt spray that he had experienced. Erik had a lifetime love affair with the sea and he was never happy unless he was out in his boat. Whenever he had the chance he was out fishing and whether his neighbours liked him or not, no one could deny that Erik was the best fisherman on the island.

He used a very simple hand line but he could always be relied on to come home with a boat full of prime fish. Other fishermen tried to avoid him; it was not that he was boastful, but he took great pleasure in landing his catch that was, without fail, twice as much as anyone else's.

They all used the same fishing grounds. Other men used longer lines and more than one line, some towed the lines behind the boat, but no matter what they did they could never be upsides with Erik. There was no magic in what Erik did. He was successful because he had an unrivalled knowledge of the sea and the fishing grounds in the area and he always used fresh bait, mussels being a favourite.

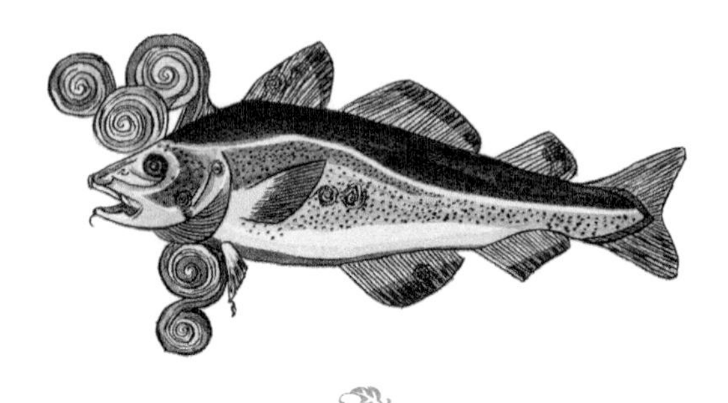

Every fisherman knew the meeds, as they were called, but Erik's great gift was to know where the fish were on any given day. Sometimes other fishermen would try to watch and see where he went.

However, on land it was a very different story. Erik had a small farm, as did many other folk who made a living from both the sea and the land. Expert fisherman he might be, but he was a poor farmer. He had no interest in the farm and his eyes were never away from the sea. His cattle were thin and scrawny and his sheep were in poor condition as well. So much so, that they often lost their wool before shearing time. His fences were neglected and neighbours often complained about Erik's stock gaining access to their crops. Whenever he was compelled to spend a day or more working on the land he would work like a madman to get the job done as quickly as possible so that he could go fishing again.

Sometimes when he was working in a field the call of the sea was so strong that he would cast aside the spade, scythe or any tool that he was using and go striding to the shore to gather bait and launch his boat.

Once, when fish were hard to find, some of the other fishermen decided to follow Erik and fish in the same grounds. Erik did not want them anywhere near him so he made a plan to fool them. He took his boat out to the nearest of the recognised fishing grounds and went through the motions of someone about to start fishing. However, he pretended that his line was tangled and he was having trouble in getting it in a fit state to fish with.

The other fishermen had long lines that take time to set and hail and Erik waited until they were committed and, without warning, took his oars and rowed away, leaving them behind. He knew that they could not follow him until they had got their lines back on board and this would allow him to get well away. Despite his years there was no man more powerful on a pair of oars.

When he got to the place where he knew that he would catch fish he stopped and put out his simple line. He began to haul in big, prime cod, the kind that makes a good price at the market.

He was aware of a big weight on his line, and looking over the side of the boat he could see white flashes from the bellies of the two biggest cod that he had caught that day. But as he continued to look down he got a glimpse of a shape underneath the cod.

It was huge and rose as the cod rose and when he could see it more clearly Erik knew that it was a monster shark. He did not know much about sharks but he knew that there was no question of catching it and taking it into the boat.

Erik had seldom experienced fear at sea but a shiver of apprehension ran down his spine when he saw that the shark was bigger than the boat. The shark showed no signs of aggression but a flick of its tail could do serious damage to the flimsy timbers of the boat.

Erik abandoned his fishing; the priority was to get ashore and away from the shark. He laid out his oars and pulled as hard as he could. After a few strokes he was two boat's lengths away from his tormentor.

Two effortless waggles of the shark's tail and this giant fish was alongside again and Erik knew that he had no chance of outpacing it. From the back of his mind came the thought that while really big sharks had lots of straight-line speed they were slow to turn. He had been told this or he had read it but, whatever, it was time to put it to the test. The shark seemed to be intent on rubbing along the side of the boat and there was once when it tipped the boat over until it was almost taking water on the other side.

Erik put a big effort into his rowing and when he had reached full speed he rapidly changed course while the shark continued on in a straight line. It was no time until the shark altered course and came alongside again.

Again Erik changed course and gained a temporary relief from the attentions of the fish but it was only temporary and soon it was back threatening the boat. Steering a zigzag course was never going to work for a number of reasons: Erik was a long way from the shore and not only were the changes of direction tiring but it meant that he was rowing twice as far he would going directly. He had to think of something else.

Before the shark arrived on the scene Erik had made an excellent fishing so he threw out a big cod. The shark paused; he

seemed to smell at the cod before eating it and resuming his pursuit of the boat.

This had earned Erik a few precious yards of freedom so he threw out another titbit for the shark. The same thing happened again and Erik began to weigh up his chances. He was setting the number of cod that he had against the distance he had to go and decided that it would save him.

What he did not bank on was that the shark got fed up with the cod; he was quickly losing interest in them. Instead of taking a close look at them and sniffing at them, he now either gobbled them up or ignored them.

Erik summonsed his last remaining reserves of strength and skill and he threw out the last remaining cod to the shark. They were near to the shore and the other fishermen saw Erik throwing out the fish.

They understood his plight but they had no sympathy for him – most of them thought that he was getting what he deserved. They were interested in seeing Erik coming home with an empty boat.

They all crowded down to the shore to watch the drama unfold and to see Erik taken down a peg. In the boat, Erik had come to detest the shark. It had ruined a day's fishing, it had endangered his life and taken him to the brink of total exhaustion. The worst bit of all was the humiliation of coming ashore without a fish to his name and he knew that he would have to endure the sniggers and gloating of the rival fisherman. The shark kept station with the boat and Erik looked at it with hatred in his eyes and vengeance in his heart.

As he rowed at frantic pace a plan hatched in his mind. He had one more trick up his sleeve. Instead of following the fairway that led into the pier he headed for the sand bar at the harbour mouth. Folk on the shore thought that he must be mad and waited to see him get wrecked and broken by the hard sand.

But Erik knew something that they did not know and neither, of course, did the shark. There was a narrow gap in the ayre, the boat could pass through it – just – but the shark a few yards to one side could not and it was stranded on the sand bar unable to get free and back into deep water.

Quick as a flash Erik stopped the boat, turned and went back into the gap. He reversed an oar and lashed his tully, his large sheath knife, on to the handle and, from a safe distance, stabbed the shark until it was stone dead.

For a time he was slumped over his oars, resting and getting back his breath. After landing he sent a young boy to the shop and told him to tell the shopkeeper that Erik wanted to see him.

In the meantime some other men arrived late on the scene. When they saw the dead shark they wondered if they could salvage it, claim it and perhaps make money from it. Once again Erik was one step ahead. When those men took a closer look they found that Erik's baler, bearing his initials, was lying on top of the shark. This showed that the shark belonged to Erik and according to the laws and customs no one could touch it without Erik's permission.

The shopkeeper acted as an agent for fish buyers and curers and Erik often did business with him. When he arrived he asked Erik why he had been sent for.

'Is that German fish buyer still here?' Erik asked.

'Yes he is still here,' was the reply.

Erik told him about the shark and asked if the German would be interested in buying it.

'He certainly will be interested,' said the shopkeeper. 'It is exactly what he would want to buy and he will pay a big price. As well as anything else the shark will provide him with a great many barrels of valuable oil.'

After a few moments thought Erik said, 'Perhaps you would like to buy it for yourself. If you buy it for yourself you can sell it on to the German and make some profit for yourself. You are an honest man and you have always paid me a fair price for my fish and I would like to see you make some money out of this shark.'

The shopkeeper thanked Erik and invited him to come to his shop so that they could agree a price for the shark. Two of the watchers at the harbour followed at a discreet distance; they were so curious to know how much the shopkeeper was prepared to pay.

They and their friends were green with envy on seeing the thick wad of notes that was passed into Erik's hands. Erik made his way home, feeling much better and with a look of satisfaction on his weathered face.

In the evening, when Erik was looking out his kitchen window, he saw a number of fishermen standing in a circle. He knew that they were talking about him and he knew that they were not saying that he was a poor fisherman but they were telling each other that he was a really bad farmer. With that Erik went to bed – it had been quite a day!

33

The Boy That Came From the Ground

When it was time to cut peats the first job was to clean the moor: it was necessary to take off a layer of earth to expose the peat. In some places this was only a thin layer, in other places it could be a foot deep.

One man who was at this work in South Yell made a startling discovery. There was a deep crack in the moor. There was nothing unusual in this, it was called a rivek. However, when he put his spade in the earth to cut a turf a voice came from the ground.

'Mind me head, mind me head!' it shouted.

Out of the rivek came a small boy perhaps eight years old. But he was no ordinary boy; he looked totally different from any other boy that man had ever seen and he was all covered in hair. He took hold of the boy and asked, 'In the name of the Lord boy where do you come from?'

'Never mind, never mind, let me go, let me go, let me go,' the boy's voice rose to a scream.

'I will not let you go, you are sure to be hungry.'

'I am not hungry,' said the boy. 'I ate a crip of heather and the black bull's bladder.'

'Where do you come from?' asked the man.

'I'm from the Knowes of Troilashoull. My place is from the Knowes of Troilashoull to the Grey Steen of Stourascord.'

The man told him that he was talking rubbish. He took the boy home with him and gave him a drink of warm milk. The boy drank the milk but as soon as it touched his stomach he was sick. The boy was angry.

'You are trying to poison me and I will not stay here very long. If you don't let me go at once I will blow my breath like the North Wind and I will take the house down around your ears. I am not a boy I am a fairy changeling and my home is in North Yell between the Grey Steen of Stourascord and the Knowes of Troilashoull. There is where I live and there is where I am going and I was only here to have a sleep.'

The boy went to bed and he snored at such a pitch that the man and his wife thought that they would have to leave the house. Another night came and the same thing happened. In the morning the boy asked again, 'When are you going to release me? If you don't I will take down the house and all your premises. It is only folk like you who can take hold of me. I tell you again I travel all over Yell but my place is from the Grey Steen of Stourascord to the Knowes of Troilashoull in North Yell, on Yinnick Staicks.

'If you let me go now then good and well but if you don't I will put a curse on you, I will kill every one of you and everyone belonging to you.'

The folk of the house knew that there was no point in keeping the boy against his will so they let him go and they never saw him or heard of him again.

34

The Poisoned Sixpence

Tamar and Hansie were childhood sweethearts. They both belonged to the same part of North Yell. They had grown up together, gone to the school together and played together. As teenagers their friendship turned into an earnest romance.

One night when they walked home together in the moonlight they pledged their troth to each other. At the time, Tamar was sixteen and Hansie was eighteen. They made a solemn promise to each other that they would love each other always and have no others.

They knew full well that they were too young to marry and they had no money and no way of getting money. However, their romance continued for the next two years. It was then that Hansie realised that if he was ever to have money he had to go the same way as hundreds of other young Shetlanders. He had to go to sea.

The usual practice was that an established seaman, home on holiday, would take a young man away with him and help him to find a job on a ship. Hansie said goodbye to a tearful Tamar and they made a fresh pledge that they would marry when Hansie returned.

Sailing ships could be at sea for a very long time but whenever Hansie had the opportunity he sent a letter home to Tamar and a letter to his parents. This went on for two years and, eventually, Hansie fell out of the habit of writing home.

His mother would ask Tamar on a regular basis if she had heard from him, but the answer was always no. They had no way of knowing if he was still alive but Tamar's faith in him never wavered and every day she hoped to hear word. She waited for him for eighteen years. By this time her hopes of hearing from Hansie had faded. She was now thirty-six years old and she reasoned that if she was ever to get married it had to be soon.

She became attracted to a man called James who came from another part of the island. He was at a New Year dance and he asked Tamar to dance with him several times during the night.

After that he came courting and Tamar welcomed his approaches and the time came, after another two years, that he asked her to marry him. She consented and plans were made for the wedding.

Twenty whole years had passed since Hansie had seen Shetland last and he felt very guilty that he had lost touch with all the folk home that loved him, especially his mother and Tamar.

It was a slack in the world of merchant shipping; his ship was lying idle in Leith with the captain wondering where his next cargo was coming from. Hansie decided, now or never, that he would take the plunge and go home for a visit.

He got a passage on a packet that took him to Lerwick in Shetland. After a few days he found a boat that was going to the north isles of Yell and Unst. It was late in the afternoon when they tied up in the port of Mid Yell.

In those days there were few roads and no transport – he had to walk the twelve miles to the north of the island. When he came in sight of his own neighbourhood there were few lights to be seen. He assumed that most folk had gone to bed.

The first house that he came to was where his best friend lived and he had no hesitation on going inside and shouting. He was seriously tired after the long walk and he knew that even if the hour was late he would still be met with a welcome.

He was not wrong in his assumption. Everyone got up; they lighted lamps and prepared food. They could not believe that he had returned after being away for twenty years. He got the sad news that his friend was dead, that he had been lost in a fishing accident.

After some time he cautiously asked about Tamar and he remarked that her house was brightly lit.

'It is the contract night,' he was told.

His host told Hansie that Tamar had decided to get married and that this Saturday night was the contract night: the night when the bargain was sealed, the night when the bridegroom was formally accepted as a member of the family and when he promised the father that he would be a dutiful husband to his daughter.

The wedding was to be on the Thursday. This came as a shock to Hansie but, when he thought about it, he could hardly complain – he hadn't made contact in twenty years, he could expect nothing else.

He made his way to his own home and once again he had to waken the household. He was saddened to learn his father had died while he had been away but his mother and his brother were both at home and well.

They were surprised and delighted to see him and, in every way, he was treated like the prodigal son. The subject of Tamar and her forthcoming wedding was sure to come up. Hansie's mother said that she sure that when Tamar heard that he was home she would ask him to the wedding.

'I think it would be for the best if she never asked me,' he replied.

But his mother proved correct, an invitation duly came and he agreed that he would attend. The marriage ceremony took place in the local kirk and the wedding company repaired to the bride's house for the wedding feast and the reception.

As the bride entered the house the wedding brunnie was broken over her head as was the custom. The brunnie was a very big oat cake and the thousands of crumbs that came from the breaking of it was the equivalent of confetti.

Everything went exactly according to plan. After the feast the dancing began. Again as custom dictated the newly married led the dancers in the Bride's Reel and the fiddler played the tunes with great energy and verve.

After a few dances Hansie got up and crossed the room to where the bride was sitting and he asked her to dance with him. She agreed and she well remembered the many times that they had danced together in the past.

They were both excellent dancers and Tamar felt that, in some measure, the years had been ruled out, but all that had to remain in the past. It was also a custom that at the end of a dance for the dancers kissed each other.

Hansie kissed Tamar and when their lips and mouths came together he transferred a coin from his mouth to hers. The coin was a sixpence and when Tamar saw it she drew back and looked at Hansie with the utmost dismay and anger.

'What did you do that for?' she demanded.

Hansie gave no answer. He went out the door into the night and Tamar took a seat as far away from her husband as she could get. The rest of the night was very tense and when it was time for everyone to go home, Tamar sent James to his own home.

Tamar and James never lived together, they never had any further contact as long as they lived and Hansie went away soon afterwards, probably back to sea. He was never back in Shetland again.

35

Black Eric of Fitful Head

A legendary sheep thief lived in the south of Shetland. He was known as Black Eric of Fitful Head. Fitful Head is a very high, steep cliff and it seemed that Black Eric was the only man who could climb it with ease.

But Black Eric was no ordinary man. No one knew who he was or where he had come from. He was a huge man and very dark skinned. He had arms that were so long that they were out of proportion to the rest of his body.

He had long black hair that had never been combed and hung around his shoulders. He wore animal skins and carried with him an iron staff. It had a heavy knob on one end and on the other end a vicious-looking sharp hook.

Black Eric was fleet of foot. He had no need for a dog as he could, with ease, run down any sheep that he wanted to capture. Often he would take two sheep in a raid, tie their feet together, thread his staff through and carry them on his shoulder.

How he was able to walk down the sheer cliff was something that local folk could not understand and no one attempted to follow. Black Eric was more than a handful for anyone on the top but the cliff face was his environment and to tackle him there was suicide.

Many local folk believed that Black Eric was in league with the powers of darkness. They believed that a njuggel helped him in his evil ways. The belief was, locally, that the njuggel transported Black Eric and his stolen sheep safely down from the cliff top to the cave where he lived.

All this would account for the blue flashes of light that fishermen reported seeing in the cliffs at Fitful Head and nearby. Black Eric was frightened of no one and he was sometimes seen in the daytime. Quite often, in the summertime, he would sleep outdoors but always with his staff placed in such a way that it could not be touched without wakening him.

The area around Fitful Head is rich farmland, the best land in Shetland. The people that Black Eric was stealing from were farmers who owned large numbers of sheep. The loss of a few sheep in the course of a year did not impact on the farmers financially but they resented the fact that they were feeding an outlaw who was also a thief.

One of those farmers was called Sandy. He was a young married man with two beautiful daughters little older than babies and they were the apples of his eye. Sandy was a hardworking man, who took great care of his farm animals. He was a peaceable man who never quarrelled with anyone but he bitterly resented the fact that Black Eric was stealing from him regularly. His farm was nearer to Fitful Head than any other farm in the parish and it was the easiest target for the outlaw.

Sandy gradually became obsessed with the determination to get even with Black Eric, either to kill him or bring him to justice. Sometimes his wife would notice the way that he was brooding, seldom speaking to her or their children and losing sleep.

Things came to a head on the day that Sandy discovered that two of his best young ewes had been taken. They were young and Sandy had selected them to be mothers of his flock in the future.

Sandy's wife could read his thoughts and she put her arms around him and tried to sooth his temper and dark mood. She suspected that he was going out to look for Black Eric and have it out with him and she was fearful for the outcome. She begged him to think of her and what would happen to her and the children if anything should happen to him. He replied that nothing was going to happen to him until it suited God to take him.

He said that he was tired and hungry and that he wasn't thinking about Black Eric at all. With that she had to be satisfied and after their meal they all went to an early bed. Sandy dozed and slept lightly and, after a good hour, when he was sure that his wife was sound asleep, he rose from the bed and got dressed.

Sandy was in the prime of life and he had confidence in his own ability and he was not afraid of Black Eric or anyone else in a fair and even fight. Some of his neighbours said that Sandy never knew his own strength but because he was such a mild-mannered man it was never obvious.

He left his house and climbed to the top of Fitful Head and quietly made his way to a place that was a favourite resting place of Black Eric. It was a rock that was shaped like a seat. By this time Sandy's eyes had become accustomed to the faint light and his pulse quickened when he saw the outlaw sitting slumped on the rock.

Sandy stood motionless for a time studying the outlaw. He looked more like a gorilla than a man and Sandy was certain that he was asleep. His iron staff was lying on the ground near to his feet.

Sandy crept forward, his shoes made from cowhide making no sound on the soft earth. His last few rapid strides took him right in front of Black Eric and he picked up the iron with his left hand.

Black Eric wakened with a fearful roar and launched himself at Sandy. Sandy met him with a powerful punch that knocked the outlaw flat on his back some distance away. Before he could launch himself again, Sandy shouted at him to stay where he was.

Holding up the staff he told Black Eric that without the staff they were even, man to man. He also told him that he was going to be killed and that he would have no more use for the staff.

So saying, with a mighty heave, he threw the staff over the high cliff. Black Eric said nothing but his ugly face was the epitome of evil and demonic rage. In a slouching gait he advanced again, and again Sandy punched him to the ground.

Back came Black Eric and this time he eluded the punch by changing direction and he was able wrap his long, powerful arm around Sandy's waist and the two men fell to the ground. What followed was a desperate life and death struggle within a few feet of the cliff edge. The outlaw, with a cunning look on his face, suddenly shifted his grip to hold Sandy around his legs just above the ankles. Back on his feet again it was clear what he intended to do: to swing Sandy around and throw him over the precipice, but in the nick of time, and with a superhuman effort, Sandy managed to get one of his feet clear and kick Black Eric in the stomach with all his strength.

The grip on his other leg loosened and Black Eric fell backwards and disappeared over the edge of the cliff. While Sandy gathered his senses he listened for a splash in the waters below but no sound came. He rose to his feet and looked over the edge of the cliff and to his horror and amazement Black Eric was only about four feet below the top of the cliff and clinging onto the spur of a rock.

With incredible strength, speed and agility he bounded back to the cliff top like some great cat. Sandy was caught unawares and before he had time to react Black Eric had him by the throat in an iron grip.

Sandy reacted by gripping Black Eric's forearms and he crushed the strength from the arms. When Sandy felt the grip on his throat slackening he pulled the outlaw towards him and grabbed him by the throat.

Sandy was a very powerful man and he was incensed by the wild ferocity of the thief. So tight was his grip that he felt Black Eric weakening, his eyes began to bulge and his tongue was protruding.

With a feeling of triumph Sandy knew that he had his enemy at his mercy; he had won the battle and he had it in his power to finish off Black Eric once and for all. Just then there was the sound of hooves and a black horse came galloping towards them.

At lightning speed it circled the two fighting men. Every time that its hooves touched the ground there was a flash of blue light and the last thing that Sandy could remember was the dizziness that came over him. When he woke up he was alone lying on the soft grass near the cliff.

There was no sign of Black Eric or the black horse but there were plenty of signs of the fight that he had been in. A heavy dew had fallen, his clothes were damp and he was feeling cold in the early morning sunshine.

He slowly made his way home and when his wife saw him she fainted; she was so sure that he had been murdered and that what she was seeing was his ghost. When she came round he managed to persuade her that he was unharmed but she said that she had seen a raven and she was sure that it was a sign of bad news to come.

Sandy was very reluctant to tell her what had happened that night – he always said that it was of no importance – and after a time she stopped asking him. Months passed and it was quite clear that Black Eric was still to the fore. However, he never took any more of Sandy's sheep.

It seemed that he had learned respect for his nearest neighbour and he was far less confident and he moved around the parish with far more caution. But he still stole sheep because it was what he lived on.

One day, Sandy was out riding on his horse and looking among his flock of sheep. The path he chose took him close to the place near the cliff edge where he had had the fight with Black Eric.

The figure of a man lying prone on the ground caused him to rein in his horse. To his utter amazement it was Black Eric himself and he appeared sound asleep. Sandy dismounted and led his horse forward to take a closer look.

Black Eric was indeed sound asleep and he was clearly unaware that anyone was close to him. He was lying flat on his back with his iron staff under his head. Sandy was surprised at this because it looked exactly like the staff that he had thrown over the cliff.

Black Eric's knees were slightly bent and Sandy was able to pass a rope underneath and fasten a running loop. This done he leaped on his horse just as the outlaw wakened and jumped to his feet with a roar of fury.

Sandy had a firm grip on the rope and as soon as the horse started forward Black Eric's feet were pulled from under him and he was dragged along, unable to resist. Sandy spotted a crew of fishermen on their way to the beach so he went towards them.

They were delighted to see that Sandy had captured the thief and they immediately surrounded him, tying his hands firmly behind him. They offered to take him to Lerwick, the capital of Shetland, to be handed over to the authorities to stand trial.

But that could not be done that day so it was decided that his hands would not be released and he would be locked in the fishermen's store until the following day. Meanwhile Sandy returned to the cliff and recovered Black Eric's staff.

He had done more than anyone to bring Black Eric's life of crime to an end and he wanted to take the staff as a trophy. This he did and put it in his barn. The fishermen who had volunteered to guard Black Eric went back to the store every hour to see that he was still secured.

As well as his hands being bound he was tethered to a post that was one of the roof supports. Every time they came within earshot Black Eric demanded that they loosen the cords tying his hands together.

Sometimes he was shouting and cursing, other times he was moaning and pleading, but the message was the same. The cord was so tight that it was causing him severe pain and closed off the blood flow to his hands.

When two of the men came in they discussed the situation and being kindly, humane men, they agreed to look and see if what the outlaw said was true. But knowing him to be very dangerous they took the precaution of locking the door behind them.

The moment that the rope was eased Black Eric slipped his hand through and was free. He violently shoved the men out of his way, sending them sprawling on the floor. He charged the door at full tilt.

The wood of the door was old and dry and it was flimsy in the first place. Black Eric went straight through it, the old door splintering like firewood, and he was away. The two fishermen got up from the floor and gave chase.

They had no hope of outrunning the outlaw but they kept him in sight. To see him heading for the cliffs was no surprise and he disappeared over the edge. When the fishermen looked over the cliff they saw Black Eric making his way down.

He seemed to be intent in following a route too difficult for ordinary men. They watched him rounding an overhanging corner; to do this he had to step down, with one foot, on a narrow ledge.

They saw his foot slip and his hands lose their grip on the rock and Black Eric fell. He struck the rocks below with a sickening thud, bounced off and slid into the sea and disappeared beneath the waves.

The fishermen took an easier route down and they waited for a long time but Black Eric never reappeared. They went back to the village and reported that Black Eric was dead and that he would never again steal sheep.

Some were sceptical; they did not accept that their enemy was finally gone. Men checked their flocks on a daily basis but there was no more sheep stealing in the area and no more was Black Eric a threat either to man or beast.

Time went on and Black Eric, while never forgotten, was not talked about every day. Folk were pleased to get him out of their minds. That is until the watermill needed repairs done to it.

More than anything it needed a spindle and this proved to be a problem because the local blacksmith had no piece of iron suitable. Sandy was a user of the mill and was as keen as anyone to get it working again.

Suddenly he remembered Black Eric's staff. He had not looked at it in months and when he did he found it to be a bit rusty but it was the perfect diameter for the spindle required, so he gave it to the blacksmith to fashion for the purpose.

The mill was restored and, as it happened, it was put back into use on Halloween night. Mills were often used at night – the burn supplying the water would be dammed first thing in the morning so the water had all day to build up.

On this first night of the reconditioned mill all was done, the miller and his son had filled the hopper with grain and the sluice gates were opened and the water began to turn the millstones. At that very moment there was a loud noise like thunder, followed by a low moaning sound. The lamp that the millers had lit suddenly went out and a terrifying vision of Black Eric in all his malevolence appeared on top of the moving millstone and pointed down at the spindle that had been made from his staff.

So terrified were the millers that they fled from the mill and never returned. When this story was told, no one would dare to go anywhere near the mill, especially at night. And so it was that the unused mill became a memorial to the outlaw, Black Eric of Fitful Head.

36

The Eagle and the Child

It was a beautiful summer morning and a young mother on the island of Yell was ready to go outdoors to milk the cows. Her infant daughter was lying in her cradle and she thought that to take the child outdoors on such a lovely morning would be good for her.

She wrapped the child in a white shawl and took her in one arm, her milking pail in the other, and went to where the two cows were tethered. The morning dew had evaporated, the air was sweet with the smell of new cut grass and there was a hint of the tang of the sea.

The mother laid her baby down on the grass close to where she was going to milk the cow. The baby was quiet, either sleeping or enjoying the outdoor experience. With one cow milked the mother moved on to the next one. It was not far away but it meant that she was a little further from the child.

All of a sudden there was a loud swoosh of huge wings, the enormous wings of a white-tailed sea eagle. Before she could move, the eagle swooped down and, firmly gripping the shawl by its talons, it flew away with the baby.

She screamed with horror but she did not panic. There was no chance of catching the eagle, albeit that the eagle carried the baby with difficulty; the weight of the child was at the limit of what the eagle could carry.

The mother ran as fast as she could to get to higher ground but all the time never taking her eyes off the flight of the eagle. In those days there were many places around the coast of Shetland where eagles regularly nested.

She reasoned that the eagle would take her child to its nest; it was just a case of knowing where. Her keen eyes were able to follow the flight as the huge bird flew in a south-easterly direction and she was able to keep it in sight long enough to know that it was heading for the Blue Banks on the island of Fetlar.

The Blue Banks are very high cliffs and a place known to have eagles' nests. She ran home to find her husband and tell him the terrible news. He immediately ran from house to house, gathering a crew to man a boat.

They lost no time in rowing to Fetlar and scouring the cliffs for any sign of the eagle. After a time one of the men spotted something white and when they were as near as they could get they all saw that it was the end of a shawl, the shawl that the baby was wrapped in.

What was equally clear was that there was no way of climbing that sheer cliff from the bottom; the eagle's nest was more than one hundred feet above the sea. They took bearings, mentally marking the place where the nest was and then rowed to a beach that was near to a township.

They made their crisis known and immediately a young Fetlar man volunteered to go down to the nest on a rope's end. No one wanted this brave young man to risk his life but he said that they had plenty of strong rope and he was light. He further argued that it was the only chance of getting back the baby. The boat's crew, the mother of the baby and numerous Fetlar men made their way to the cliff top and they were able to pinpoint the ledge that the nest was on.

The young man was lowered down on a strong, heavy rope but he had, in his hand, a lighter rope to be used for signalling. One tug on this rope meant that he wanted slack on the heavy rope and a series of sharp tugs on the heavy rope meant that he wanted to be pulled up again.

The ledge with the nest proved to be quite broad and the young man, being brave and sure footed, gave one tug on the rope. When he got to the nest the eagle was absent, maybe it was looking for food for the chicks.

They were quite big and, with the baby in the middle of the nest, they were standing on either side looking down at the newcomer. The young man never hesitated; he did not fancy getting to grips with the adult eagle. He threw the two eaglets out of the nest and picked up the child and tugged urgently on the signalling rope. Willing hands pulled him up but, as he reached the top, the eagle was seen flying in fast towards the nest.

She made angry noises but she went down to sea level and picked up first one, and then the other of her chicks and returned them to the nest. No one was concerned for the welfare of the eagle or her eaglets – they were only concerned for the child.

To the relief and delight of everyone the baby was unhurt and the young man was proclaimed as a hero. The two families kept in touch and twenty years later the same young man and the girl that he rescued from the eagle's nest got married.

There are folk in Shetland, even now, who can trace their ancestry back to that couple.

37

The Minister's Meeting

At one time in Shetland the most important and senior minister was Mr Fascal who lived in his manse in Tingwall, not far from the site of the Norse parliament. He held the title of moderator and he was responsible for all the other ministers in Shetland.

To make sure that everyone was up to speed with his doctrine and thinking he called a meeting several times a year. The meeting was in Mr Fascal's home and he prided himself on the hospitality that he showed to his fellow clergy.

To make sure that they were well catered for, he gave his housekeeper a generous sum of money and bade her go to the town of Lerwick and buy quality tea and sweetmeats to serve.

The meeting consisted of a total of twelve ministers including Mr Fascal himself. He sat at the far end of a large oval table and each man had the necessary papers and a candle in front of him.

Jane, the housekeeper, served the tea and biscuits and it was soon obvious to everyone that, instead of being the best, the fare set in front of them was of the most inferior quality. The tea was scarcely drinkable, the biscuits were soft and none of it was plentiful.

One of the older men remarked that what they were eating and drinking was not up to Mr Fascal's usual standard. That august gentleman was mortified; he knew that Jane had bought the cheapest she could find and he rang a bell and summonsed her into his presence.

When he confronted her she freely admitted that she had spent most of the money on herself. The oldest minister was the one who showed the most anger. He said that she had to be in league with the Devil, and he would come and take her to hell.

Mr Fascal said that the Devil would never take away anyone from his house and that the Devil held no terrors for him. No sooner had he spoken the words then there was a great gust of icy cold wind through the room. The papers were blown off the table and the candles were all blown out except the one in front of Mr Fascal. He had shielded the flame from the wind and by its light they could all see that the Devil himself was in the room.

'I have come to take Jane away from here,' he roared. 'She has been a good servant to me and she has no future here.'

'Your very name is an abomination: it is composed of words that emphasise what you are. You are an il, vil, evil Devil and I will defy you.'

The Devil was furious. He drew himself up to his full height, showing off his pointed ears, his sharp horns, red eyes and red face. His spear-like tail hung down below his coat and he stamped his cloven hooves on the floor.

'Jane is mine and I will take her!' he thundered.

With the exception of Mr Fascal the ministers were afraid and they sat with heads bowed, awaiting the outcome of this clash of wills. Mr Fascal cleared his throat and shouted in a clear, steady voice:

> Jesus the name over all,
> At hell or earth or sea,
> Angels and men before him fall,
> And Devils fear and flee.

On hearing this, the Devil howled as if in pain and he did, indeed, flee. He made a pass through the stone wall of the building, scattering the stones as if they were made from paper.

The Devil effectively wrecked that house and it was never repaired and the undamaged parts of it fell into ruins. Nor was the Devil finished with his revenge on Mr Fascal: he put a curse on him. He decreed that no matter where Mr Fascal went the wind would always blow in his face. In some ways this was a big disadvantage, but it was a great advantage in a boat. If he sat facing the stern then they always had a fair wind.

The Devil further declared that Mr Fascal would die neither on land or sea and that prophecy was accurate. One day, when he was on his way to preach on a different island, he died suddenly when his boat was half in and half out of the water.

38

Singna Geo

In the one thousand-mile coastline of the Shetland Isles there are hundred of geos (a gully or an inlet from the sea). Some are easy to climb down while others are under high cliffs with steep sides.

Shetland is a place that has no trees so any driftwood is considered valuable. Shetland men, whenever there is an onshore wind, are forever beachcombing in the hope that the sea has brought a bounty.

One North Yell man spotted a bundle at the bottom of Singna Geo, from the top he could not make out what it was. Singna Geo has quite high cliffs but to climb down is not too difficult.

Having got to the bottom he made his way through the large boulders to the object that he had seen from the top of the cliff. To his horror he discovered that it was a human body, partly decomposed.

He made no attempt to move it but hurried home to tell his wife and family and to enlist the help of some of his neighbours. A number of men went back to Singna Geo and they took with them the door of an outhouse to use as an improvised stretcher.

Gingerly they rolled the dead man on to the door and it was carried up the steep path to the top. In those days men had great respect for the power of the sea and a belief in the sea gods.

They believed that when the sea had claimed a life the sea gods would be angry if the body was taken away from the sea. Men were so dependent on the sea for their livelihood that it was unthinkable to do anything that might offend the sea gods.

Nonetheless the man's body could not be ignored, so, as in other such instances, the men buried it as close to the shore as possible.

Just before the burial they had a closer look at the corpse and they could see by his dress that he was a seaman. They also noticed a small bundle, wrapped in a brightly coloured handkerchief and tied around his neck.

The men talked about it and speculated about what might be in the bundle but none of them touched it. It was embedded in their culture and upbringing that to steal from the dead was among the worst sins that anyone could commit. The grave was filled in and the men made their solemn and thoughtful way home.

Most of them were able to get on with their lives but the man who found the body was greatly troubled by nightmares. The ghost of the drowned seaman appeared at his bedside with the bundle around his neck. Every night his plea and message was the same. He was complaining that the place where he was buried was wet and uncomfortable.

He was also saying that if the man went back to his grave, lifted the body and reburied it in a better place he would find, tied around his neck, enough gold that would be good pay. The man knew that the grave was not in an ideal place but it had to be a compromise. It had to be near the sea and it had to be a place where the digging of a grave was possible, it was a rocky area. The nightmare kept recurring but, tempted as he was, the man made no attempt to move the body.

Instead he took a spade and drained the area. He made ditches that took all the surface water down the slope to the sea. This seemed to satisfy the ghost because it never reappeared again and the man was able to sleep without any more nightmares.

No doubt the body is still there, with the bundle, but the grave is unmarked and it is unlikely that anyone knows exactly where it is.

39

The Death of James Smith

James Smith was a prosperous man. He had made money from fish curing and from the property that he owned. He had started off working for another but he was greedy and ambitious so he set up his own business and proved to be ruthless and unscrupulous. He was hated by the fishermen who worked the boats that he owned; he made sure that they never made enough money to buy the boats for themselves, and he never allowed them to sell fish to anyone but him and it was he who fixed the price.

As he made money he invested it again and, in time, he made enough money to build a grand house to live in. But no matter how rich or notable a man is, the time comes when he has to die, and so it was with James Smith.

When an important man died it was the custom, in those days, for two ministers to 'wauk' him. That is they sat with the corpse until the funeral. Smith had been a church member and supporter, and so it was that the Revd James Gordon and the Revd James Ingram were at Smith's house to keep watch.

The two ministers were in the drawing room examining a family bible while the dead man was laid out in a room adjacent. The hour was late and the house was silent when suddenly there came a loud knocking noise from the alter room. Ingram, being the senior of the two ministers, ordered Gordon to go and find out what had caused the noise. Gordon refused; he admitted that he was too frightened.

'I would go into that room if the Devil himself was there,' Ingram declared. He picked up the twin candlestick and pushed open the room with Gordon on his heels. The corpse was sitting up and they watched in disbelief as the strap that prevented the jaw of the dead man from dropping, untied itself. The corpse spoke: 'I have been a dreadful sinner and I can't get rest for my soul until I have revealed certain things that trouble me. I did not ask for a repentance before I died. Will God forgive me at this late hour?'

Gordon was the first to find speech. 'You could have asked before now but all things are possible with God.'

The dead man spoke again: 'I want to tell you some of my worst sins. I evicted Ossie Tait from his land and took his farm for myself. When I bought a fat cow from a tenant I cheated him of thirteen shillings because he could not count English coin. I sold the widow Marion Jamieson's two sons to the Press Gang; I told them where the boys were hiding. Will God forgive me?'

Gordon repeated that all things are possible with God but he should have asked sooner. The dead man seemed to think that he had, indeed, been forgiven. He lay down again and never moved again.

This strange story was told far and wide and later, when the Revd James Gordon attended a large gathering of ministers and church officials, the moderator asked him about the incident. Gordon told them of the experience that he and James Ingram had had.

'We are not going to debate whether the days of miracles are past but I can hardly get my head around the story you are telling.'

This raised some anger in Gordon and he demanded to know if the moderator was calling him a liar. The moderator said that he would not call a fellow minister a liar but wondered if perhaps there was some optical illusion or something in his brain that made him believe such a thing

When James Ingram arrived later in the day he was asked if he recalled this happening. He told the moderator exactly the same story as Gordon.

'If two holy men, men of the cloth in their right sight and senses, tell the same story then I accept it as being words of truth,' declared the moderator.

James was left to rest in peace by the clergy but one who never forgave him was Marion Jamieson.

The treachery of James Smith meant that she had lost her two sons. They were all she had left since she had also lost her husband. Her grief was terrible to see and she hid herself away to become something of a recluse.

However, her neighbours and her few friends knew that she practiced witchcraft. She sat down in her barn, loosened her hair, fasted for several days, and said over and over again, 'Vengeance is mine, I will repay.' Although James Smith was dead, he had left behind him a wealthy family and it was on them that Marion Jamieson put her curse: 'Their fine, big, fair mansion house with all the servants – the walls will be turned into a dunghill and the birds of the air will have the stones for a resting place, ten coffins will leave the house within days.'

And so it was that the Smith family died out and when one dead coffin left the house another corpse was being measured for a coffin. It was said that there were so many coffins that they rattled one on top of the other. In time the roof was off, the doors rotted away and animals sheltered in it and birds built their nests in what was left of the walls.

40

Sigmund of Gord

There once was a fiddler named Sigmund and he lived on the west coast of the Shetland Mainland at a place called Gord. Like every other fiddler he was much in demand at every social gathering.

Of course he did not get any pay for his music; it was what every fiddler was expected to do. He and his family lived on a croft (smallholding) and made a frugal living from working the land and some fishing.

One afternoon, Sigmund went to fish from the rocks and had considerable success. His basket was so full of fish that he had to rest on the way home. He took the basket from his back and placed it behind a large rock.

While he sat resting he heard music coming from a hillock nearby and when he went closer to listen, the hill opened and it was light inside. The tune being played was new to him and he was curious to know who the fiddler was.

When he went in the opening closed behind him and he could see no way out again. It became clear to Sigmund that this was a place where the trows lived and they were having a great party.

As well as a fiddler playing, dozens of trows were dancing and drinking and making merry. They seemed to know that Sigmund was a fiddler because he was soon involved in the playing and at first he really enjoyed himself.

Eventually he knew that he should go home to his family and the trows thanked him for playing for them and they opened up the hillside and allowed him to leave. They also said to him that he was to keep the fiddle that he had been playing and look on it as a gift from the trows.

It was pitch dark outside but he knew the area like the back of his hand and he was able to go to the big rock and pick up his basket of fish. When he pushed open the door of his home he was in for a shock. There was no one there that he knew, he was among total strangers.

'Who are you and what are you all doing in my house and where is my folk?' he demanded.

He was in for another shock when he saw his reflection in a mirror. He was a very old man with a white beard, he was dressed in rags and he was still carrying the fiddle that he had got from the trows.

In response to his questions he was greeted with howls of laughter from the household, especially the younger ones. The man of the house, the grandfather was sitting beside the fire smoking his pipe.

After some thought he asked Sigmund who he was. Sigmund told him and said that he had been fishing; he had played a few tunes on the way home and implored the grandfather to tell him what was going on.

'There was a man with your name that lived here but that was a hundred years ago. He went fishing one night and never came back, they thought that he fallen into the sea and been washed away.'

'Where is my folk then?' asked Sigmund.

'Your folk are all dead and we are no relation to them, we came here when this croft became empty and we have been the tenants ever since.'

'If my folk are all dead the best thing I can do is go and join them.'

So saying, Sigmund turned on his heel and went outside again. One young man in the house had never laughed at Sigmund, he felt sorry for this old, confused, man. Besides he was also a fiddler and he was interested in the fiddle that Sigmund carried.

He followed Sigmund outside and watched him walk up though the yard at the back of the house to the boundary wall where there was a well. He stopped and put the fiddle under his chin and played a tune that the boy had never heard before.

That done, Sigmund collapsed. The young man found the remains of a man that was little more than dust and the tiny fiddle beside him. But the young man had a great ear for music and he was able to remember the tune that Sigmund played and fiddlers know this tune to this day.

41

The Woman with the Red Hand

A man walking through the hills of the Shetland's north Mainland was horrified to stumble on the body of a woman that he knew. He guessed that she had not been dead for very long.

The woman was known as a very hard worker and it was assumed that she had collapsed; perhaps she had some sort of a seizure. Many a time folk had said that she should take more rest.

She was local and she had a husband and family. The man who found the body was very distressed but he had to go to the dead woman's house and tell them the bad news. A number of men were gathered and they helped the husband to carry her home.

The corpse was laid out in the traditional way, awaiting a coffin. When it arrived from the undertakers they had the neighbours in to pay their respects. The minister was with them to say a prayer before the body was put into the coffin and the lid nailed down. The entire company was shocked when they discovered that the corpse was still supple.

It had been in the same place for three days and there were no signs of rigor mortis. Nonetheless she was lifted and laid in the coffin. In those days coffins were made locally and often from rough wood. When the woman's body was being placed in the coffin one of her arms fell to one side and one of her fingers was torn on a nail point or a splinter.

Some declared that she was seen to flinch and show signs of pain and her finger began to bleed. Her husband wondered if she really was dead. He suggested that perhaps she was in a coma or in a trance and he wanted to delay the funeral to see if she awoke.

Time went on and nothing changed; the dead woman showed no signs of life but she remained flexible in all her joints. Eventually the husband sent for the minister again and he agreed that the woman had to be buried – they were sure that she was dead.

The funeral went ahead in the time-honoured way and the husband was faced with getting on with the rest of his life the best way he could. However, when winter came there were disturbing reports of a number of folk seeing a ghost.

It was always in the same place near the burn and many were so scared that they would not leave their homes after dark. Everyone who saw this ghost all told the same story: it was the woman who never became stiff after death.

She had a red hand as if it was covered with blood and she seemed to be saying that she was in pain because of her injured finger. When the husband heard of this he was very distressed and went to see the minister.

He asked the minister if there was anything that he could do to lay this ghost to rest. The minister was angry and accused him of dabbling in witchcraft and being in league with the Devil and he told the poor man in no uncertain terms that he was having nothing to do with it.

More distressed than ever, the poor man went home, beside himself with grief and worry. One of his neighbours told him of a man in another community who was expert in 'laying ghosts'. This man was consulted but he was reluctant to be involved. However, fully appreciating the distress of the widower he agreed to go to the area where the ghost was seen. He made no promises but he said that he would do the best he could to put matters right.

When he was taken to the place where the ghost was last seen he asked to be left by himself. The widower sat with his friends in his cottage – there was no question of going to bed until the 'ghost layer' returned from his vigil.

Late in the night he returned, looking calm and serene. When he was asked if he had met the ghost, he nodded.

'Did you speak to her?' he was asked. Again he nodded.

'What did you say?' was the next question.

'What I said to her and what she said to me is between me, her and God and no man will ever know what was said. But I can tell you that she is now at rest and you will never see her or hear her again.'

That man died of old age and went to his grave without ever discussing the subject again. And the woman with the red hand was never seen again.

42

The Snuff Taker

A very long time ago a man called Thorwald was lost to the sea. He was well known in the community as a stern, tough man but one who was wise to the ways of the sea and the cliffs. He always wore leather sea boots that were handmade and he also wore a smock and a Southwester hat.

His family and friends looked for him for many weeks but eventually they gave up hope, they knew that it was impossible for him to have survived. He was never forgotten and his mysterious disappearance was spoken about by many generations to come. Around three hundred years later, his ghost appeared.

Hakon was a trapper and a hunter. He made a living from killing animals for their pelts and from killing animals that were vermin and a pest to farmers. He always carried a pistol with him.

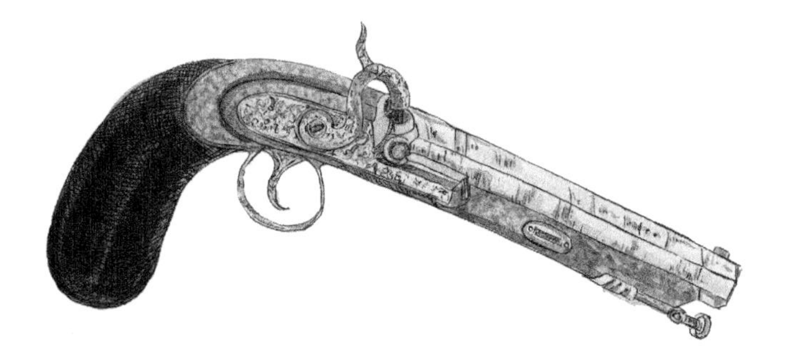

Sometimes he caught, in his traps, an animal big and fierce enough to fight back so he used the pistol to dispatch them. One night when he was walking home he met the ghost. He was on a narrow path; far below him was the cliff and the sea, above him was a steep, high, hill.

It was poor visibility, mist and drizzle, but when this figure loomed up in front of him he knew immediately that it was not a real person. He saw the smock, the sea boots and the hat: no one that he knew wore clothes like that.

He had heard about Thorwald and he knew that this had to be his ghost. He also thought that it was evil and he guessed that it was likely to do him harm. If there had been any way of avoiding the ghost, Hakon would have taken it.

It was not an option to leave the path; he had no choice but to meet the ghost face to face. Using all his courage he spoke and asked the ghost what he wanted.

'I am Thorwald,' the ghost said in a chilling voice, 'and I have walked the shore and the hills for hundreds of years because I have to find someone to tell my story to.'

Hakon did not want to hear the story and he turned away to go back the way he had come. But the eerie voice came again.

'No matter how far you go I will follow. There is no escape for you until it pleases me to release you.'

Hakon's brain was working overtime. Then he remembered his pistol and wondered if he could shoot this ghost. It crossed his mind that perhaps this being would see the drawing of the pistol as a hostile move and attack him.

He reckoned that Thorwald would never have seen a pistol in life so, with a bit of luck, he would not recognise it as a danger. Hakon remembered something else that he had heard about Thorwald: he was addicted to snuff.

Cautiously, Hakon drew the pistol from his belt; it was loaded and ready to fire.

'What is it you got there?' asked the ghost.

'It is an instrument used nowadays for taking snuff. Would you like to try it?' asked Hakon.

Without waiting for an answer he put the muzzle of the gun under the ghost's nose and pulled the trigger. There was a mighty explosion and a flash of fire and when the smoke cleared the ghost was still standing there but with a contented grin on his face.

'That is the best snuff I ever had,' he said.

Thorwald's ghost had enjoyed the shot so much that he was in a really good mood. He never did Hakon any harm but he insisted on telling his story and Hakon had to listen.

43

THE THREE YELLS

Lowrie was a crofter who lived in a house that was built on a hillside overlooking the voe (in Shetland, a voe is an inlet of the sea; in Scotland they call the same thing a sea loch). Lowrie's neighbour and best friend Brussie lived on the other side of the voe.

One day came the sad news that Lowrie's friend had died. Lowrie visited the house to see Brussie's widow and he was also a pallbearer at the funeral. Lowrie missed his friend and he thought about him every day, just as they had been in the habit of speaking to each other every day.

One night Lowrie had a dream; he dreamed that Brussie was sending for him. The dream said that he should go to Brussie's house at midnight and take his mare with him. The mare was a work animal that pulled a cart and did any other job that had to be done.

Lowrie tried to ignore the dream but the same dream came for three nights in succession and the dream was exactly the same every time. Lowrie knew that he had to do something about it. Instinct told him that he would never be rid of the dream until he did what he was told to do in the dream.

He knew exactly how long it would take him to walk around the head of the voe and, leading the mare on a tether, he arrived at Brussie's house at midnight sharp. No sooner had he paused than Brussie appeared in front of him. At first Lowrie was too shocked to speak but when he tried Brussie signalled for him to be silent.

'We have very little time,' he said. 'We have been friends all our lives and I wanted to tell you that your wife is unfaithful to you. She is having an affair with another man. Now go home as fast as you can. Go on the mare's back and make her gallop. On your way you will hear three yells and if you fail to get in the door of your house before the third yell is heard then you will be a dead man.'

Lowrie wanted to ask questions but Brussie had already disappeared so he got on the mare's back and set off for home. The mare was rather old and not given to speed. However, the tide was out and this allowed a shortcut at the head of the voe.

As they went down the slope to the sea the first yell came. It was not very loud nor was it very frightening but Lowrie urged more haste from the mare as he went through the ebb stones.

As they commenced the climb up to Lowrie's house the second yell came. This time it was louder and it had a certain ring of menace and Lowrie was sweating with fear; he never doubted the truth of Brussie's warning.

The poor old mare could go no faster and Lowrie was in a desperate race against time. He was relieved to see that the door of his house was open and he rode the mare straight at it. He flattened himself down on the mare's neck and the mare was too tired to swerve or even stop.

The dreaded third yell came but by that time Lowrie, still on the mare, was inside; the lintel of the door was behind him. However, the hindquarters of the mare were still outside and she, poor brute, dropped stone dead.

44

The Funeral Ghosts

The village of Quarff never had its own kirk and kirkyard until 1828. The kirk built then was the work of the famous engineer Thomas Telford. Telford was a Scotsman and he is best known for the construction of the Caledonian Canal.

Before this kirk was built, Quarff folk, when they died, were buried at St Lawrence kirk on Burra. This involved a crossing over Cliff Sound. Quarff is a place where the Shetland Mainland is narrow and through some trick played by the Ice Age the valley runs east–west rather than the usual north–south.

Cliff Sound is not very wide but there were occasions when the crossing was rough and difficult, yet in consideration for the grieving families at the time of a funeral the boatmen made maximum effort to cross on the appointed day.

After one funeral, on a stormy day, the boatmen from Quarff failed to return. That night, a Quarff man awoke from his sleep in the middle of the night. He saw three men come through the window and stand on the floor of his bedroom.

He was so astonished and frightened that he was unable to speak. The men did not speak either and there was total silence. After a short time the three men left in the same way that they entered.

A day or two after, the same three men appeared to a crofter who also lived in Quarff. Again he never spoke to them and the ghostly trio were equally silent. In another area of Quarff the same three men appeared once more. This time the man that saw them spoke and the three replied. One stepped forward and said, 'Thank you for speaking to us. We cannot speak unless we are spoken to.

Our bodies were never found and our souls cannot rest until our families know what happened to us. Both before and after the funeral we were given too much strong drink. On the way back, in the middle of Cliff Sound, we had a quarrel. The sea was rough and the boat was swamped. We lost our lives in the most witless manner and since then we have wandered, waiting, and hoping, for someone to speak to us.'

With their story told the ghosts could find peace and they were never seen again.

45

The Skull

Hakkie was a young man who was in the very best of spirits. It was the Saturday night before his wedding and he was on his way to collect the proclamation, the wedding banns, from the Session Clerk and deliver them to the minister for reading out in the kirk the following day.

In his village, the graveyard surrounded the kirk and the manse was nearby. Hakkie took a shortcut through the graveyard and he was somewhat surprised to see a human skull on the path in front of him.

Undaunted, and with reckless disrespect, he kicked the skull out of his way. That done he felt somewhat guilty and without really knowing what he was doing, he picked up the skull and spoke to it: 'It is my wedding this week and I invite you to come.'

It came as a hammer blow to Hakkie when the skull spoke back to him in rebuke:

> Remember man as thou pass by,
> As thou is now so once was I,
> As I am now so thou shall be,
> Remember man that thou must dee.

With shaking hands Hakkie put the skull in the place that he believed it had come from.

This graveyard was full and it was the practice to bury coffins in graves that had been used already. Any skeletons or bones that had to be dug up were stored among the grass cuttings and re-buried at a convenient time.

Very shaken he went on his way and met his best man.

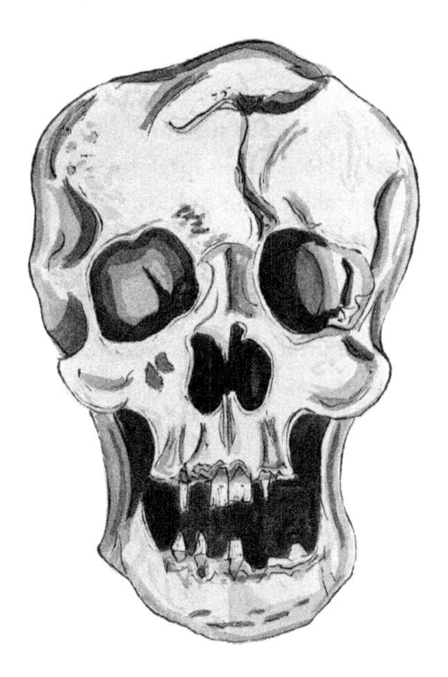

Together they saw the minister and collected the necessary paperwork. The minister's wife gave them tea and biscuits and the minister said a prayer and gave Hakkie his blessing.

It was quite a long walk to the bride's house and the best man knew that there was something troubling Hakkie. They had been close friends for all of their lives and eventually Hakkie told his friend about the skull but made him promise that he would tell no one else.

At the bride's house they all went through the formalities of offering a dram from the spüring bottle before settling down to an evening of eating and drinking and the 'contract' cementing the wedding; all went according to plan.

In the days before village halls, the wedding feast was usually held in the bride's house. Everyone invited gathered there after the wedding ceremony in the kirk. A large, but thin, oatcake was broken over the bride's head, the scattered crumbs symbolising fertility. The ben room of the house had been cleared for the dancing and a fiddler was placed in the corner.

In the middle of the night there was a knock on the door. Doors were never locked and anyone coming to a house simply walked in. When the door was opened they found a total stranger standing on the doorstep. He asked to speak to the bridegroom. With a feeling of unease Hakkie went to the door. The stranger pulled him outside and closed the door.

'Who are you and what do you want?' asked Hakkie.

'Don't you remember that you asked me to your wedding? It was my skull that you kicked in the graveyard.'

Inside the house the wedding guests thought that Hakkie had been a long time with the stranger but when they looked out there was no one to be seen.

Hakkie tried very hard to get rid of the stranger. When he was free he opened the door of the house but he knew, at once, that something was very wrong. There was no sound of the fiddle or of feet dancing or voices, it was all as quiet as the grave.

The only person he saw was an old woman lighting the fire. He asked her what had become of the wedding company. She did not answer for some time but she eyed him up and down in his wedding suit. Then she said, 'There has been no wedding here for a very long time but my grandmother told me of a wedding where the bridegroom disappeared with a stranger and never returned. That was one hundred years ago.'

Hakkie knew then that he had been severely punished for kicking the skull in the graveyard. He had not been away for a few minutes as he had believed but away for a hundred years. With that knowledge he collapsed into a small pile of dust.

46

Norway's First Troll

Shetland has sixteen inhabited islands and around another eighty or so that are uninhabited. The biggest of the islands is called simply the Mainland and it is here that most of the population live.

In the middle of the Mainland there is a long, lonely stretch of road that runs through a valley. The hills on either side are called 'da Kames' and there is no one who lives in the valley. No one, that is, except the trows.

The trows are the little people, the fairies, and they live in places all over Shetland, but the Kames are home to many of them. The trows seldom trouble people and they love music: they sing, dance and play fiddles. They have a darker side too, they have magic and their revenge on anyone who wrongs them can be quite severe.

However, once upon a time, they shared the valley with a very easy-going giant. He was rather dull, slow and stupid and the trows had him for a playground. The giant was a farmer but anytime that he lay down to sleep the trows would come to molest him. They found this great fun.

They would get into his hair as if they were in a jungle; they would go into his ears. Two of them would lift one of the giant's eyelids to check that he was sleeping. Sometimes they crawled up the legs of his trousers; how far up they ventured is not known but it is said that they left no stone unturned and no avenue unexplored.

But their favourite entertainment was to climb on the giant's forehead and slide down his nose to land on his upper lip.

The giant ignored this as best he could but one night he felt that he could take no more so he decided to expel the trows and put them in a place where they could not annoy him.

The giant made a giant straw basket called a kishie. It is usually carried on the back and this one was so big that more than three hundred sheaves of corn were needed. The trows watched him at work and they became more and more fascinated and came closer and closer to see exactly what he was doing.

This was where they made a big mistake, because he was able to scoop them up by the dozen and imprison them in the kishie. The giant tied the top tight so that none could escape and went on the prowl to round up any stray trows that were at a distance away.

Satisfied that he had captured every last trow, he reinforced the top so that it was entirely secure. The giant tried to put the kishie full of trows on his back but it was too heavy. The weight of one trow was nothing to the giant but when there were hundreds of them together they weighed a lot.

In his attempts to lift the kishie the giant staggered and his right foot came down on the earth with a clash, leaving a giant footmark, and his knee came to earth as well. In time the holes filled with water and are there to be seen to this day as small lochs. The footprint is called Pettawater and anyone passing along the road can see it and it shows that the giant only had two toes. The other, where his knee landed, is called Kneefel.

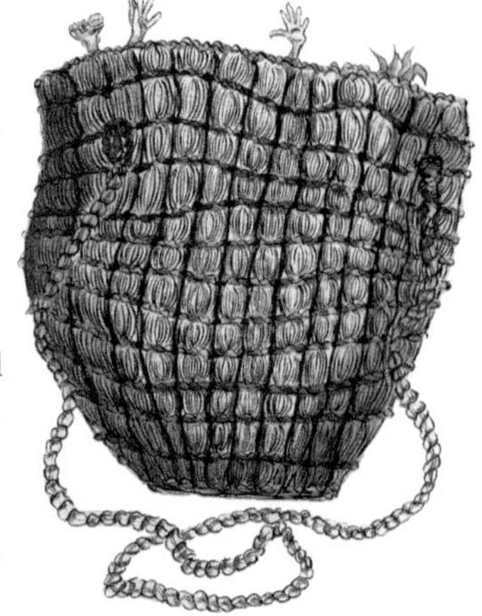

The giant was dismayed to find that he could not carry the kishie but he was determined to deport the trows to Norway. He reasoned that Norway was so far away that they would not come back again.

Unable to lift the kishie he dragged it along the ground, but straw is a soft material and soon a small hole appeared on a corner. The hole was big enough for the trows to escape through and as the hole got bigger they all escaped.

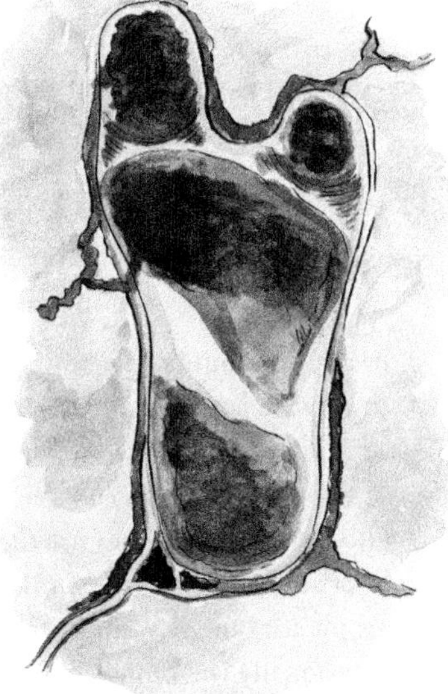

When the giant reached Norway he was furious when he saw that the kishie had no bottom and it was empty of trows. So angry was the giant that he lay on his knees and cursed and swore and beat the ground with his hands,tearing out vast quantities of earth.

Those deep trenches filled with water and nowadays they are very beautiful and known as the fjords of Norway. When the giant calmed down he looked around and he realised that Norway was the most beautiful country that he had ever seen and so he decided to stay there.

After all, he reasoned, there were no trows in Norway to trouble him. And so it was that he became the very first Norwegian Troll and why Shetland still has trows.

47

Midwife to the Trow

In any community the howdy wife was a most important person. In a large community there might be several howdie women working together or individually. Someone describing the duties of a howdy wife once said that they are there when someone comes into the world and they are there when someone leaves the world. In other words they were midwives, but they also prepared dead people for burial. Some of them had a mystic air about them and occasionally the hint of witchcraft, causing some folk to look on them in awe.

When called to assist a birth, a howdy wife would never tolerate the presence of a man in the house. Men were told, in no uncertain terms, to go and not return until after the birth. Of course, some howdie women were more highly regarded than others and therefore more in demand.

One such woman was at home looking after her house when a knock came to the door. This was most unusual; in those days no one locked their door and anyone visiting simply walked in. It was dark out but she could see a very small man who stood outside her door and she knew, instinctively, that he was a trow.

She invited him in and he said that he needed her help. He explained that his wife was in labour and had been for some time and she needed expert help to give birth. The howdy wife put on outdoor clothes and they set off to where the trows lived.

The howdy wife knew about trows, everyone did, but she did not know where they lived or how they lived. Outside they walked through the village and as her eyes grew accustomed to the darkness she was aware of passing familiar landmarks.

After a time she was seeing a landscape that she did not know; they were in a place totally strange to her and she began to feel uneasy. The trow reassured her that no harm would come to her and she could trust him to take her back.

At last the trow led her into a house and into a bedroom where the trow's wife was lying in the bed in a state of great distress. The howdy wife took off her coat and examined the woman and she could see why the birth was so difficult.

Using all her skill and experience she managed to bring the child into the world and the father was so very grateful. He gave the howdy wife a small bag filled with gold coins and offered to escort her back to her home.

By this time the daylight was coming in and the howdy wifecould see her surroundings more clearly. There was no doubt she was in a place that she had never been in before. After what seemed a long walk she began to see, once more, things that she did recognise.

The trow halted and asked if she knew where she was. She nodded. He asked if she was sure that she could find her way back to her own home and again she nodded. Without another word he took from his pocket a small jar.

He removed the top, dipped in his finger and smeared a small amount of ointment in both her eyes. When she blinked to clear her vision the trow had disappeared and when she looked back there was nothing but the village and the places that she had known all her life.

Rather bemused she made her way back to where she lived but the experience of being the place of the trows was a memory that was always foremost in her thoughts. Many a time she retraced her steps and walked in the same direction as the trow took her. No matter how far she walked she never saw any trace of the place where she had been to deliver the trow baby. In time she got on with her life as it had been before she had the encounter with the trows.

The long winter passed and with it the long dark nights. Summer was a busy time for everyone with fishing, agriculture and a host of other things as well. One summer task that involved everyone was the day that the sheep were all rounded up to be shorn.

Shetland sheep have very soft wool and they sometimes shed it naturally. It can be pulled off the sheep and clippers are unnecessary. This can be done by men, women and children, and as well as being a job of work it was something of a social event.

A peat fire would be built and women would boil billycans for tea making. Many would enthuse this tea tasted better than any tea that they had at home. The sheep were all crowded into a large pen and taken out one by one to get the wool taken off.

The howdy wife was there too and when she looked into the pen she was astonished to see the trow in among the sheep. He was not that much taller than the sheep but there was not the slightest doubt he was the very same trow that had asked for her help.

He was wearing loose trousers and a tunic with a tight belt around the waist. A bag was hanging from the belt and the trow was stealing wool. From every sheep he was taking a handful of wool and stuffing it into the bag.

She did not mention this to anyone else because it was clear that no one else had seen him and if she raised a hue and cry the folk would think that she had gone mad. She watched and waited and when the trow had the bag full of wool he left the pen.

She made her way around so that she was close to him and then spoke.

'How is your wife and child, the one I delivered?' she asked.

'They are doing well,' he answered, 'but how did you know that I was here?'

'I can see you.'

'Can you see me from both eyes?' was the next question.

The howdy wife experimented by closing first one eye and then the other.

'I can see you with my left eye but not the right,' she told him.

The trow then stood to his full height, took hold of her shawl and pulled her down until their faces were close together. He then blew into her left eye, causing her to blink. When she looked again she found that she could see nothing from her left eye. She could not see the trow or anything else; she was blind in that eye for the rest of her life.

48

KATIE LOTTIE

Katie Lottie was a lively nine-year-old girl who spent the long summer days wandering the hills and the shoreline with her dog Berry. All the time spent outdoors gave Katie a big appetite and she often visited her grandmother, who always seemed to be baking and preparing food.

One day she was aware of a delightful smell coming from Granny's kitchen and she knew exactly what it was: it was Granny baking brünnies – her favourite food. Brünnies were big, round, thick oatcakes and Katie loved them with or without butter.

Granny gave her one so newly baked that it was still warm. Katie went outside to sit on a favourite rock to enjoy her oatcake. Berry was there too and Katie shared the brünnie with him, but when it was finished she was still hungry.

She was given another one but Granny tut tutted indulgently, saying that Katie was a bottomless hole where food disappeared without trace. After the second brünnie Katie was still not satisfied and she asked for one more to eat as she walked home.

This time she was given a small one and when she was outdoors once more she realised that she was not hungry anymore and decided to keep the brünnie for later. Running down the hill she accidentally dropped the brünnie and, being round, it rolled on its edge faster than she could run.

There was a wall at the bottom of the field and Katie expected the brünnie to crash into the wall and break into small pieces. However, the brünnie suddenly disappeared and when Katie looked there was a hole in the ground that was partly covered by grass.

Katie thought that all she had to do was to put her hand in and take it out. She reached in but the hole was so deep that she could find no bottom. She lay face down but her arm was far too short; it was a very deep hole.

Katie sat up and lowered her feet into the hole. She was curious to know what else was in there besides her brünnie. She found that she could lower herself down and she found steps and hand holds. When she reached the bottom she found that she was in a kind of tunnel and light was coming from the far end of it. However, when she looked back the way that she had come there was no light to be seen and the way that she had entered seemed to be closed up.

Katie Lottie was not frightened. She saw this as a big adventure and walked on towards the light. Through an archway she came into a beautiful meadow. The grass was the greenest that she had ever seen and the flowers were so exotic that she hesitated to put down her feet, in case she harmed any of them.

Katie loved flowers and she really enjoyed the wild flowers that grew everywhere in the summer. But these flowers were different, they were all new to her; she had never seen any of them before.

There were trees too. There are no trees in Shetland and this was the first time that she had ever seen a tree. Some had hanging branches and she was able to touch the leaves. Up ahead was another archway and corridor so she walked through that as well.

In the corridor she could smell food cooking, and coming into another area she saw an enormous pot hanging over an open fire. She also saw a giantess on the far away side of the pot and, for the first time, she felt frightened.

The giantess saw her too and she reached out a very long arm and, with the forefinger and thumb of a huge hand, picked her up. Katie found herself looking closely at the biggest face that she had ever seen.

Examining Katie, the giantess said, 'Karl will be coming home soon and he will be hungry. This will be a morsel of meat for him.' But looking again at Katie she added, 'You are just a rickle of bones but you will have to do. He likes his food stuffed so I will fill you with porridge.'

She put Katie in a basket and from there she could not escape. She could hear the giantess put oatmeal into the pot and heard the sound of her stirring it. When the giant returned home the woman asked him if he had had any luck with his hunting. He said that the only thing he had got was a small duck; there was not a cow or a sheep to be seen.

She showed Katie to him and he agreed that while she was not very big she was better than nothing. The giant was very frightening. If the old woman was ugly he was ten times worse and he had sharp teeth. Katie shuddered, terrified about what was going to happen to her.

The giant said that he would eat the duck while the porridge cooked. He proceeded to tear the feathers off the bird and devour it raw, bones and all. For a time he could not speak because his mouth was so full of meat and a bone stuck in his teeth.

Katie was given a bowl of porridge. It was a lot smaller than the bowl that the giantess had for herself, but it was huge to Katie. The spoon that she had to sup with was so big that she had to use both hands and after eating the brünnies she was not hungry.

She managed to eat the porridge but she was given another bowlful and that was too much and she just pretended to eat. Meanwhile the giantess had eaten three monster bowls of porridge and was showing signs of being sleepy. The giant got up after finishing the duck and looked at Katie again.

'She is not very big so I will go and see if I can find some turnips and potatoes, that will eek out to make a decent meal,' he said.

He went off through the trees and Katie knew that this gave her a chance of escaping. The woman was leaning over with her eyes shut and seemed to be sleeping. Making no noise, Katie got up and crept away from the fire and the giantess.

When she was near the trees she heard a sound that filled her with terror – she thought that the giantess had heard her leave and was coming after her. She need not have worried though, the sound that she heard was the old woman snoring.

Making her way through the trees was a new experience for Katie. The smell and the touch of the forest was something that was very different to anything that she was used to. At last she came out the other side and into a clearing and saw another archway and corridor.

She went through and immediately she knew that she was in a very different place and the sounds and the smells were ones that she knew very well. It was the sound and the smell of the sea.

At the far end of the corridor she came out onto a beach and looking around she saw that she was in one of her most favourite places – Selkie Geo and that is near to Granny's house. Looking back, the cave could not be seen; it had closed leaving the solid cliff face. Katie often played there and she knew the path that lead to the top of the cliff.

'Where on earth have you been ?' asked Granny. 'Berry has been seeking you and I was worried in case something bad had happened to you.'

'I have been walking along the shore,' Katie answered. She knew that it was no use telling Granny, or anyone else, her adventures because they would never believe her.

49

KIDNAPPED BY THE TROWS

John and Katie were a young married couple. In their home parish they were well known and popular, and when they had their wedding they were given many presents and received good wishes from all of their neighbours and friends.

John was a fisherman but they also had a croft. They were poor in the sense that they had little and could not afford any luxuries but they counted their blessings, especially after one year of marriage when they had a beautiful, healthy baby girl.

Katie looked after most of the crofting work: she milked the cows, hoed the fields and made hay in the summer time, and she also knitted sea boot socks for John, shawls for the baby and ganseys for all of them.

There were few spare moments but Katie enjoyed her work and took great pride in her little girl and the family life that she had. However, all that changed one summer morning while John was at the fishing.

Katie had a heap of laundry to do; it had been a spell of rainy weather and not weather to hang out clothes on the drying green. She fell to it with a will and got it all done. Before she went to hang out the washing she checked on the baby.

Little Annie was sound asleep in her cradle so she had no hesitation in leaving her; after all she would not be very long. When she came back in she looked in to see if young Annie was still sleeping; she thought that maybe she would be ready for a feed.

To her horror she found that the cradle was empty and the blanket covering Annie had gone too. Katie was completely mystified as to what had happened. Her first thought was that maybe one of the neighbours had come to visit and heard Annie crying. Maybe she had lifted her out of the cradle and taken her in her arms for a walk. Frantic, Katie ran from house to house asking if anyone knew what had happened to her darling baby girl.

No one knew anything and it was a tearful Katie that greeted John on his return at the end of the day. He had no more idea than she had about what had happened but he sat down and tried to reason things out.

'No one would steal our baby,' he said at last. 'There has to be some dark powers at work here.'

There was no sleep for Katie and John that night. The news had spread and his fishing crew knew, without being told, that he would never leave Katie that day. True he did not go to the fishing but he did not stay at home either.

'It's a long shot,' he told Katie, 'but I am going to see the howdy wife.'

Katie was too distraught to argue and as soon as he had finished a frugal breakfast he set out to see the howdy wife, old Merran, who lived about four miles away. Every parish in Shetland had one or two howdie women.

Howdie women acted as midwives; indeed, it was Merran who brought Annie into the world. Howdie women were also the ones who prepared any dead person for burial. They were accredited with being wise women, to the extent of having knowledge of witchcraft.

When John arrived at her house old Merran was in no way surprised to see him. She gave him a warm welcome but she was very crippled and could only get around the house with the aid of a stout stick.

'I was expecting a visit from you, John. I heard what had happened to you and if I had not been so cripple I would have come to see you.'

She asked how Katie was and then she addressed the purpose of John's visit. She asked many questions and John was impatient to find out if Merran had any answers.

'Do you think that the trows have taken our baby?' he asked.

'I certainly do,' she replied. 'And it would not be the first time that they have done such a thing.'

She went on to explain, 'The trows have powerful magic and they can look after themselves very well, but there is one thing that they cannot control. For some unknown reason they always had a shortage of girls. They never produce enough baby girls to ensure that their race will continue. Four out of five babies born are all boys and so the trows feel the need to steal baby girls from humans.'

Merran said that sometimes the trows were so desperate that they would steal adult females if they were of childbearing age. One man who was in the hills working at his peats overheard the trows plotting to steal his wife. He was able to foil their plans because he knew that it was going to happen.

'Can you do anything to get back our baby?' John asked.

'Yes, I can, and I'll tell you what you must do,' said Merran. 'You should go to the sea and take a bucket of water from breaking seas. You must take three stones from below the high water mark. Heat the stones in the fire and put them into the seawater. That done they have to be turned three times with the sun and three times against the sun before passing them three times through the flame of a peat fire.' She also gave him incantations to say.

'Do as I say John and soon you will have back your beautiful baby,' she ended.

John made his way home, hardly daring to hope that there was any truth that Merran's instructions would have any effect. He told Katie and they decided that it was the only hope they had, so it was worth a try.

The waves were rolling onto the beach and John got the bucket full of salt water. He did not care that he was soaked in the process. They carried out Merran's plan to the letter and they both crouched down beside the fire to carry out the last part.

They had a lively fire, with the flames leaping high, and when they passed the third stone though the flame for the third time they heard a soft sound behind them. When they looked around, there was Annie lying contentedly in her cradle and none the worse for her time with the trows.

It was the last time that they ever left Annie by herself and they never had any more trouble with the trows, but John, Katie and young Annie made a visit to Merran's house to thank the old howdy wife for the miracle that she had worked.

50

FEEDING THE TROWS

Especially in the autumn and early winter, Shetland men often went fishing from the rocks. This was called going to the kraigs. They fished for young coal fish known as sillocks and bigger ones called piltocks.

This was done partly because it was tasty food and partly as a recreation; after a hard day's work it was therapeutic to sit at the shore and catch plentiful fish. The best time of day for this was when the light was beginning to fade and a keen fisherman would stay until it was almost dark and the fish stopped taking the lures.

In the hamlet of Gloup there was a man called Maunsie Spence and he was on his way home with a basket well-filled with sillocks and piltocks. He lived quite a long way from the shore and he sat down for a short rest.

His place of rest was a very large stone, perhaps twelve feet long, four feet wide and two feet thick. It was known as a place where the trows lived. There are many stories of men hearing music on their way home from the kraigs. The trows are very fond of fiddle music and many Shetland tunes are said to come from them.

Maunsie did not hear any music but what he *was* acutely aware of was a sharp pain in his ankle. He got up and limped home. The pain eased to an ache but his ankle was so uncomfortable that he could not ignore it for a moment.

He knew that it was a trow who had struck him a blow with a little hammer that they used and he knew why they had done it and what they wanted. He limped home and set about gutting and washing the fish ready to cook for the supper.

The fish was boiled and Maunsie told his wife to keep the brø, the water that the fish was boiled in. Maunsie and his family enjoyed a delicious meal of boiled sillocks, piltocks and young potatoes with the melted fish livers poured over.

After he had finished eating, Maunsie poured the brø into a big can and set off back to the big stone where he had rested. His ankle still ached but not so bad that he could not walk.

He walked all the way around the stone, pouring out a little brø as he went and as he did so the pain in his ankle lessened and by the time that he shook the last drops out of the can the pain had gone entirely.

Maunsie smiled to himself, he had been right, the trows had a craving for sillock brø and now that they had got some they released Maunsie from his pain. He was able to stride home fully restored.

51

WINYADEPLA

On the east side of the island of Fetlar there was a watermill and it was called Fir Vaa. Grinding grain was always done in winter because in Shetland there are no rivers and no plentiful water to drive a mill. With the rain and possible melt water in winter some of the streams are powerful enough to do the job.

Mills were owned by communities so when the conditions were right there were numerous families all needing the mill at the same time. This meant that often the mill was used at night as well as during the night.

There was a small building beside Fir Vaa that was used for storing straw and it would be a place for a miller to rest while the mill was grinding. A miller might even sleep among the straw, as after filling the hopper with grain and setting the mill going there was nothing more to do. A miller always knew if the hopper was empty because it made a different noise when it had to be refilled.

Not everyone fancied the idea of being at the mill alone because there had been reports of trows visiting the mill.

One man who had no fear of the trows went there boldly. It was night time and dark with just a measure of moonlight. He was a big powerful man and he carried several bags of grain there on his back. There was no wind, the mill was silent and the only sound was the waves lapping gently on the nearby shore.

After the mill was in motion and he was satisfied that everything was working as it should, he went into the building next door and bedded himself down, snuggling among the straw to enjoy the rest and a pinch or two of snuff. After a time he dozed off but became wide awake when he heard a familiar sound coming from the shore.

It was the sound of a boat's keel striking the shingle beach as it landed. He got up and looked out the door. The moon was a bit brighter now and he could see quite clearly a number of trows stepping ashore. It was not uncommon for boats to be stolen by the trows, although they usually brought them back.

The trows trooped up from the shore and they were heading straight for the mill. The man was not quite so brave now so he went back into the building and retreated into the furthest corner and covered himself with as much straw as he could. He hoped that if he made no noise they would never know that he was there, but as soon as they came into the building one of them said, 'We'll not trouble the sleeper, he is not a bad man and we can play him a tune.'

One of them had a fiddle and they played the same tune over and over again while the rest danced. This went on for a very long time and the miller heard the tune so often that it was firmly planted in his brain.

When the trows were aware of the first signs of dawn they left, but the miller stayed where he was until he heard the keel of the boat scraping once more on the shingle. When he looked out he could see the boat leaving the shore.

By this time the mill was long finished grinding so he stopped it, bagged up his meal and headed for home. The family thought that he had been far too long away and they were slightly worried.

He assured them that he was fine and he told them of his encounter with the trows. At first they laughed at him but he said that he could prove it. His son was a fiddler so he told the boy to fetch the fiddle.

'You know that I have never composed a tune in my life but I have a tune that the trows have given me. I know it is a tune that you have never heard before.'

He hummed the tune over a few times. It was rather a simple tune and the boy soon picked it up and before long he was playing it freely. It became a popular tune in Fetlar and fiddlers all over Shetland learnt it.

At first it was known as 'Old Gibbie's Tune', Gibbie being the name of the miller. The tune is still popular now but it is called 'Winyadepla'; this is the name of the loch that supplied the Fir Vaa with water.

52

The Borrowed Boat

In days long ago, almost every household owned a boat. The boat would be the responsibility of the man of the house. Some women were good at rowing and boat handling but it was nearly always men who went to sea.

A boat was very useful; it was used as a carrier, a means of transport from one village to another and for fishing. People depended on the sea to provide a vital part of their income and food.

It was an unwritten law that no one interfered with another's boat. The only exception was if the boat was in danger, then someone, in the area, might be able to save it. But it was unthinkable that anyone would use another's boat without permission.

It was December and all the boats had been, with the onset of winter, taken well clear of the sea and secured, propped up and tied down by heavy stones at either end. During a Shetland winter the weather seldom allowed fishing to take place.

One man who was out feeding his sheep and passing close to the beach was aware of something not quite right with his boat. When he took a closer look he saw that it was not secured in the same way as he had left it. Indeed, all the evidence suggested that the boat had been used. The most telling sign was a fresh grove in the beach that the keel had made when it was launched and drawn up again.

The crofter found this astonishing but he put everything back to rights again and resolved to check on his boat more often. A few days later there was more evidence of the boat being used and no one in the community had asked permission to use it.

In the weeks that followed the same thing happened again. He was certain that someone was using his boat. He decided that the only way to get to the bottom of the matter was to keep watch.

On a December night, to keep watch in the open was a cold uncomfortable business, so he stepped into the boat and lay down near the bow and covered himself with a piece of canvas that had once seen service as a sail.

The crofter made sure that he had a peephole so that he could see anyone who came to the boat. He made himself as comfortable as possible and settled down to wait. The wind fell away until it was flat calm, and the moon rose to shine from a clear frosty sky. The only sound came from the sea lapping on the shore.

He did not have very long to wait before he heard the crunch of boots on the shingle. He hardly dared breathe but he saw small hands deftly untying the rope at the bow and the stern.

When he got a better view he saw that the users of his boat were trows, the little people. There were three of them, all small males, and he was amazed at the ease with which they were able to pull the boat down to the water's edge.

They launched the boat; one trow sat on the seat nearest the bow of the boat and manned two oars, the other two sat in front of him and had an oar each. After clearing the beach the trows took just three strokes of the oars before they landed on another beach.

The crofter could not think of a place where such a short journey would take them but the trows left the boat and pulled it part of the way up the beach. The crofter ventured out from under his covering to see if he could ascertain where they were.

The moonlight was still bright and he immediately knew exactly where they were, it was a place that he knew well. But it was nowhere near his home beach, it was miles away and it would take three ordinary men hours to row there.

The crofter watched as they walked towards the cliff that was at the top of the beach. When they got near to it an opening appeared and they disappeared inside. He had been there before, salvaging driftwood, and he had never seen a cave in that cliff face.

It was not long before the trows reappeared, each one each one carrying a wooden keg. The crofter hid himself again but saw them put the kegs into the boat. One of the trows went back up the beach and returned with another keg. This done they re-launched the boat and another three strokes of the oars took them back to the home beach.

The trows took the boat up to its resting place just as easily as they took it down and re-tied the ropes. As they left the boat each of them lifted a keg and said, 'One for me.'

The fourth was lifted and set down near to where the crofter was hiding and they all chanted, 'One for the owner, one for the owner.'

The man realised that the trows had been aware of him from the start but had given no sign of their knowledge. He secured his boat in the way he wanted it and when he lifted the keg from the boat he found that it was very heavy – it was full of some sort of liquid.

He thought that he had been away for a very long time but when he got home his wife told him that he had been gone for no time at all. He opened the keg and sampled the contents.

It was brandy but of the most superior quality, miles better than any spirit that he, or his wife, had ever tasted. When Christmas came and they had visitors they were very proud to be able to offer such a beautiful drink.

The visiting men asked where he had obtained such wonderful liquor from and, rather shamefaced, he told them about the trip he had been on with the trows. When some of the younger men heard this they were determined to make the same journey to see if they could bring back some more.

The weather continued to be calm and frosty and a boat with four men set out to the beach far away where the

crofter said that the trows had taken him. This time three strokes of the oars moved them a few feet and proved to be back-breaking work to get to their destination.

They searched the cliff face but there was no opening and, reluctantly, they had to give up and return home. By the time they got to the home beach it was dark and they were all exhausted.

The crofter kept an eye on his boat but there was no evidence that the trows had ever used it again. He would have gladly gone with them again to get another keg of brandy but the opportunity never came.

53

CHRISTMAS AT WINDHOUSE

In its heyday Windhouse was the grandest dwelling on the island of Yell. It was the home of the Spence family, who had, for generations, been landlords, merchants and the local aristocracy.

One of the Spence lairds had six children, three boys and three girls. One Christmas Eve there was a disturbance outside the house. It was uncanny and everyone inside felt afraid.

It began a few minutes before midnight: there was a mighty noise like a hurricane and the house became deathly cold. The whole building shook from the foundations to the timbers of the roof. The fire went black and the moonlight could not be seen through the windows.

After a short time everything returned to normal; the fire burned bright once more and the room was warm again. The man of the house was brave enough to look out the door. The moon was shining bright and there was nothing out of the ordinary to be seen.

The following morning one of the children, a son, did not get up for breakfast and when they investigated the boy was found dead in his bed.

Another year went past as normal but on Christmas Eve at exactly the same time the same thing happened as on the previous Christmas Eve. This time it was one of the girls who died in her bed. The family could not understand why this happened. They could only hope and pray that nothing like it would ever happen again.

But it did, only this time it was a servant that died and they were no nearer to having any explanation. Three deaths in the house all at Christmas was too much for the family to bear.

Mr Spence decided that he and the remaining family members would leave the house and stay with friends when Christmas came around again. They made themselves ready, yoked a pony into a gig and loaded up all the things that they were taking with them.

At midday they all sat around the table in the dining room having a meal before they set out on the journey to the neighbouring village where their friends lived. Suddenly there was an urgent knocking at the front door and Mr Spence sent a servant to see who it was and what they wanted.

The servant returned and said to Mr Spence that he should come and speak to the man that she had taken in. He was a seaman, soaking wet and utterly exhausted, so much so that he could hardly stay upright.

The Spences found dry clothes for him, took him to the table and gave him a bowl of broth and several slices of bread. When the seaman had recovered somewhat, he said that he was a survivor of a wrecked ship and that he he had been without food for more than twenty-four hours and without sleep for thirty-six hours.

The ship had been damaged by a severe storm and the rudder was unshipped and torn away. Without being able to steer the ship it was driven helplessly before the wind. They had taken off nearly all the sails and they had tried to rig sea anchors but in the darkness the ship had run ashore into the face of a high cliff.

The ship struck very hard and seemed to rebound but the next squall of wind and the next giant wave took it straight in and it stuck fast and began to break up. The main mast broke off at deck level and fell against the cliff face.

This seaman and one of his shipmates climbed the slanting mast like a ladder and managed to get a foothold in the cliff face. Another roll and another grinding crash and the mast, that had been their lifeline, fell away and none of the other seamen could follow them.

The two men clinging to the cliff in the storm had a desperate struggle but they managed to reach the cliff top. As far as they knew they were the only survivors but they were also aware that unless they could find shelter they would not survive either.

They started walking inland. The west side of Yell was entirely unknown to them and there were no lights to be seen. After a time the two men, who were near the end of their endurance, disagreed about the direction that they should head in.

One went south and reached Windhouse the other headed north and, as it happened, he perished. He was found dead beside a wall; no doubt he had taken shelter there. At Windhouse, Mr Spence told the seaman about the ghost that haunted the house on Christmas Eve and that they were going away for the night.

The seaman said that he was too exhausted to go any further. He declared that he was not frightened of any ghost and that, if they would allow him, he would stay in the house overnight.

Mr Spence said that he was welcome to stay but warned him of the danger. By this time the daylight was fading as the Spence family left. The seaman had been shown a bed so there he rested and slept for several hours.

When he awoke he felt hungry again, so he had another meal from food that he found in the kitchen. After that he looked around the house and one of the things he found was a large woodcutter's axe. He stoked up the fire again and made himself comfortable but with the axe within easy reach.

He slept some more but became wide awake when he heard the sound that the Spences had described and the house was shaking as if it was made of paper. The fire was all but extinguished and he felt as cold as if he was out in the open.

The door was shaking and rattling as if someone was trying to get in. This seaman was a truly brave man: he opened the door and was confronted by a black mass that blotted out all light.

He attacked it with his axe but the axe did not bite in, indeed there was little resistance, but he kept hacking at it and after a time he sensed that this monster was weakening. It drifted away from the house and rose into the air.

But the seaman was unrelenting; when he could not reach it he threw the axe into the mass and when the axe fell to the ground he picked it up and did the same thing again. He pursued it and kept up the assault.

About a quarter of a mile from Windhouse the monster fell to the ground and lay still. The seaman judged it to be dead so he left it where it was, went back to Windhouse and retired to bed.

He slept soundly for many hours and shortly after he rose Mr Spence arrived back on horseback to find out if the seaman was still alive and if the ghost had visited. The seaman told him his story and advised that he should gather a team of men to bury the monster.

They went back to the place where it had fallen and found it, a black shapeless and flexible lump. It was an ugly sight in the daylight and no man had ever seen anything like it before. They dug a big hole and shovelled it in and covered it over with earth.

This place can be seen to the present day. It is covered in green grass and the many acres surrounding it is all brown moorland with heather growing on it. Never again was the house of the Spence family molested by this malevolent monster.

54

FARKAR'S PIG

It was near to Christmas but in the Farkar household the conversion was more about trows than the festive season. For some reason the trows seemed to be more active at Jül time; perhaps it was because of the winter solstice or perhaps it was that they sought the warmness of people's houses. Most Shetland homes, in the old days, consisted of just two rooms.

In the kitchen there was always a box bed. It looked more like a cupboard and it always had sliding doors. The box bed in the kitchen was where young Henry Farkar slept and his mother asked him if he was frightened of the trows.

'Not I,' said Henry. 'You have told me time and again what to say if the trows trouble me.'

Henry sounded very confident but he was a bit worried and he could not get to sleep. After lying awake for more than an hour he heard someone opening the door of the house.

No one ever locked a house door so it was easy to get in. Henry was up on his knees and there was an open seam between the boards of the sliding door. There was very little light but he could see two shapes – trows – and they were carrying bundles.

It was a man and a woman. The man went to the fire and took away the big wet peats that were there to ensure that the fire lay in all night. He stirred the embers and put on some small dry peats from the basket beside the fire.

When the fire was revived it filled the room with light and Henry could see that the woman was carrying a baby in her arms. He could also see that the child had sore eyes, as the eyelids were red and inflamed.

The man had a pig, an earthenware jug, with tight cork and a handle on the side for carrying. The woman spoke: 'Put it beside the fire so that the oil warms, it will not work if it is too cold.'

The man put the pig close to the fire and they waited. The woman spoke again, 'The peerie oolet [little rascal] in the bed will never know that we are here.'

It came as a shock to Henry that the trows were aware of his presence but he kept very still.

The woman took from a pocket a small bottle and filled it with oil from the pig. She then, very gently, rubbed a small amount of the oil on to the sore eyes of the baby. Immediately the eyes were cured, all the redness gone and the child was comfortable again.

Henry saw the man approaching the bed and, for the first time, he was really frightened and he remembered what his mother had taught him.

'Guid surround me and the pig,' he shouted.

Immediately there was a minor flash of light and an explosion and when Henry looked again the trows had disappeared – there was no one in the kitchen but himself, but the pig still stood by the fire.

His parents heard of the commotion and they got up. Henry told them all that had taken place and although he was only nine years old he claimed the pig for his own. The contents of the pig proved to be truly remarkable.

It was oil of a sort but it could cure all ills. If anyone had any problems of the skin a tiny amount rubbed on the sore place was all that was needed. If anyone had other health problems a small spoonful swallowed worked wonders.

News of this magic medicine spread and folk came from far and near to partake enough to cure their illnesses. Henry never turned anyone away; he gave a small quantity to all who asked.

In time, Henry's parents both died of old age and Henry was married and he had three daughters. Henry's wife was as kindly as he was and she gave oil from the pig to all that needed it.

By this time Henry had had the pig for twenty years and it was still full. It was truly magic and Henry instinctively knew that it would always replenish itself so long as it was never emptied, so he was always careful not to take too much out at any one time.

Henry's three daughters all grew up, got married and left home. Henry himself was getting on in years when his wife died. He was by himself for a time but eventually he got married again.

Sadly his second wife was not as kindly as his first. She had a hard mercenary streak and she adamant that Henry should sell the oil rather than give it away.

'No, no, I got the pig with the oil for nothing and it would be wrong to try and make money from it,' he said.

His wife was not convinced; she complained that so many folk came to the house that she could not get on with her work. One day, when Henry was away, she charged two women a sum of money for the oil that they got.

They were willing enough to pay as the benefits from the oil were so great that it was well worth the money. The following day another eight folk came for oil and they were also willing to pay.

However, when Henry picked up the pig he knew immediately that something was very wrong. The pig was as light as a feather and it was empty. It never gave another drop of oil. The spell had been broken by his wife's greed.

55

In Aboot da Nite

When visitors came to the house, and after tea and supper, very often storytelling started. If there were children they were often reluctant to go to bed because they were enjoying the visitors. Perhaps the mother would ask if they would go to bed if one of the visitors told them a story. Sometimes the visitor would tease the child: 'I'll tell you a story about a Tammie Norie (puffin) if you'll promise not to speak in the middle of it.' The child was in a no win situation; if they did not answer then there was no story and if they said anything they were accused of speaking in the middle of the story. Of course they always got a story in the end.

Many a time a child got a reprieve from going to bed because one story led to another and a general storytelling session would begin. Spooky ghost stories were popular and stories that had been handed down from one generation to another.

However, the most popular stories of all were the humorous and the far-fetched ones. One man told a story of the time that he was in Greenland at the whaling. He was ashore on the ice when he saw a polar bear approaching.

He had an old muzzle-loading shotgun and he took aim and fired but to no effect, the bear kept coming. He quickly put in more gunpowder and wadding but to his horror he realised that he had no shot.

By this time the bear was close and he was so frightened that he broke out into a cold sweat. The temperature was so low that the sweat froze on his brow. He scraped it off, put it in the gun and shot the bear stone dead!

Another man told of the time, also in the Arctic on a whaling ship, that he accidentally cut off his friend's head. They were on deck flensing a whale with the long, very sharp, lances. The sea was rough and the deck was slippery; he lost his balance and in flailing around he struck his friend Ertie in the neck with the sharp bit of the lance. He cut the head clean off and it fell on the deck with a thump.

Quick as a flash he picked it up and stuck it back on. After a few minutes Ertie spoke to him. He picked up his lance and carried on with the work as if nothing had happened. He seemed to be none the worse.

At the end of their work on deck they went down to the forecastle for food and warmness. There was a large cast-iron stove and the men welcomed the cosiness after the intense cold on deck.

Everything was fine until Ertie blew his nose and threw his head in the fire – he had seemingly thawed out!

'Let be fer let be,' as Robbie said to the otter. This phrase was often heard. Robbie Glen was a hunter and he was always looking for otters. An otter's pelt was valuable – it commanded a good price.

Robbie had a series of otter houses built. They were enclosures that an otter could enter but could not escape from. In themselves they were humane but what happened after that was not. Any hunter had a very healthy respect for the jaws of an otter and the sharp teeth, but an otter trapped in this way was brutally clubbed to death. One day Robbie Glen found a fine big dog otter in one of his traps. When he was satisfied that it was dead he slung it over his shoulder and, holding it by the tail, he set off for home to skin it.

However, Robbie soon found out that he had a problem. He thought that the otter was dead and the otter thought it wasn't and it sank its razor-sharp teeth into Robbie's right buttock.

Robbie had plenty of experience of otters and he knew that it would never let go until he released his grip. He let go of the tail and the otter let go of his buttock and the last that he saw of it was when it disappeared into the sea, no doubt still with a sore head.

Another man told of a giant that he knew. He was so big that he measured nine inches between the eyes and he was four and twenty knuckles from the spoon of his breast to his Adam's apple. He was no fool either; he could find his way from the house to the peat stack on a misty day and he could find hen's eggs among the rhubarbs.

Uncle Jeemie told of a day when he and his friends were off at the fishing. It was a fine summer day but after a time there were some worrying weather signs to be seen. The sky darkened and tufts of grass were blowing in the breeze.

That was bad enough, but when a divot fell in the boat they got really worried and the skipper told them to take in the fishing lines. That done they made all speed for the shore. It was a puzzle to them because the sea remained calm and the wind did not increase.

It was only when they neared the home beach that the mystery was solved. The grass, the divots and the darkened sky were the result of the rival shopkeepers playing golf!

My grand uncle Dennel had a quirky sense of humour and seldom told any kind of a story other than tall ones. He told of one, one late afternoon, when he had to round up some sheep. It was very dark and his dog was young and inexperienced, but he showed great potential.

He sent the dog to go around the sheep and bring them to him but the dog ignored him and went straight home. Uncle Dennel was angry and frustrated and he was considering what punishment he was going to give out when all the sheep came to him.

He then saw the dog looming up out of the gloom and he was carrying the cat in his mouth. Uncle Dennel then realised what had happened. It was so dark that the dog could not see the sheep so he had been home and fetched the cat. Cats can see in the dark!

He also told of a minister who used to be in North Yell. Mr Watson had lost an arm and his congregation used to help him to get a store of peat for the winter. He was in the habit of borrowing a horse and cart for bringing home his peats from the hill.

Dennel said that he saw Mr Watson, sitting in the cart, and galloping along the road at high speed holding onto his hat with the hand that he did not have!